FINANCIAL SNAKES

Paul Clitheroe is a founding director
of Australia's leading financial plann   ...as been
involved in the investment industry since he graduated from
the University of New South Wales in the late 1970s. He
has completed the two-year postgraduate course offered by
the Securities Institute and is a fellow of that professional
body. He was a board member of the Financial Planning
Association of Australia between 1992 and 1994; in 1993 he
was elected Vice President and in 1994, President.

From 1993 to 2002 Paul hosted the Channel Nine program
Money and now presents weekly *Money* segments on *A Current
Affair* with Ray Martin as well as hosting *Money* specials. Since
1999 Paul has been the chairman and chief commentator of
Money Magazine. Overall, he has been a media commentator
and conference speaker for more than fifteen years, and is
regarded as a leading expert in the field of personal investment strategies and advice. Paul lives in Sydney with his wife
and three children.

Nicola Field is a chartered accountant, who, following a career
change, completed a master's degree in education. She writes
for *Money* magazine and has helped research Paul Clitheroe's
other books, *Making Money* and *Make Your Fortune by 40*. She
lives in Sydney with her husband and three young children.

Financial Snakes & Ladders

Strategies for tough times

PAUL CLITHEROE

Written in association with Nicola Field

VIKING
an imprint of
PENGUIN BOOKS

Viking

Published by the Penguin Group
Penguin Books Australia Ltd
250 Camberwell Road, Camberwell, Victoria 3124, Australia
Penguin Books Ltd
80 Strand, London WC2R 0RL, England
Penguin Putnam Inc.
375 Hudson Street, New York, New York 10014, USA
Penguin Books, a division of Pearson Canada
10 Alcorn Avenue, Toronto, Ontario, Canada M4V 3B2
Penguin Books (NZ) Ltd
Cnr Rosedale and Airborne Roads, Albany, Auckland, New Zealand
Penguin Books (South Africa) (Pty) Ltd
24 Sturdee Avenue, Rosebank, Johannesburg 2196, South Africa
Penguin Books India (P) Ltd
11, Community Centre, Panchsheel Park, New Delhi 110 017, India

First published by Penguin Books Australia Ltd 2003

10 9 8 7 6 5 4 3 2 1

Design by Cathy Larsen, Penguin Design Studio
Cover illustration by Tracie Grimwood
Typeset in 12/16 Fairfield Light by Midland Typesetters, Maryborough, Victoria
Printed and bound in Australia by McPherson's Printing Group, Maryborough, Victoria

National Library of Australia
Cataloguing-in-Publication data:

Clitheroe, Paul.
   Financial snakes and ladders: strategies for tough times.

   Includes index.
   ISBN 0 670 04067 3.

   1. Finance, Personal – Australia. I. Field, Nicola. II. Title.

332.02400994

www.penguin.com.au

Contents

Acknowledgements

As I write this in April 2003, in the world of investment, markets seem far more interested in sliding down snakes than climbing up ladders.

But writing a book is far more akin to climbing a ladder. It is a slow, painstaking process that you take step by step, and one that would not have been possible without Nicola Field. Producing a book while looking after a young family is no simple task and I thank her very much. Thanks is also due to my old friend Chris Walker, who, as with all of my books, has been heavily involved with its final look and feel.

I would also like to thank Martine Richards for her input into Chapter 6, and thanks also to Christine Kelly, a family law specialist, for her help with Chapter 8.

Finally, I would like to thank the team at ipac securities for their technical help; my personal assistant Jodie Williamson who co-ordinated their input; and Andrew Wells, who came up with what I think is a really good book title. In my experience, wealth creation is like a game of snakes and ladders – erratic leaps up and down rather than smooth, steady progress.

Introduction

I have to admit that the idea of writing a book about surviving difficult times was in my mind well before the terrorist attacks of
11 September 2001, the share market roller-coaster of recent years,
the turmoil in the Middle East and the SARS crisis of 2003.

During this book's early conception, markets were booming
along. But history makes it very clear that a market boom will be
followed by a market bust as sure as night follows day.

It was always my intention to reinforce this point, and to alert
readers to the fact that about the only time when there are really
good buying opportunities are when investment markets fall. This
is one of the few positives about such times because, sadly, most
people buy in at the top of the market – rarely do people buy at
the bottom. Rather, they are usually in a state of panic and trying
to sell.

As I write this in early 2003, the property market is finally beginning to cool, and in some areas, turn down. Throughout 2002, I and

many others were pointing out that property was very expensive, having doubled or tripled in value, while shares were looking cheap. But what were people buying in a frenzy – cheap shares or expensive property? You've got it – expensive property.

I reckon that mass-produced 'off the plan' inner-city apartments will take a real flogging, causing difficult times for many people. But the real purpose of this book is not just to explain the difficulties caused by falling markets.

I really felt that there was a need for a book that looked at the type of things that people ask and talk to me about on a regular basis. Sad things, such as bankruptcy and divorce, or special but expensive events, such as having children. Bankruptcy, in particular, is really on the rise in our community. Rising personal debt and credit card problems will see tens of thousands of people taking this path in 2003. And in my experience, those considering bankruptcy know little about their options or the consequences. Whether or not you have ever contemplated such a course of action, this book will give you a clear understanding of the whole process.

The difficult times I will refer to in this book – falling markets, too much debt, divorce, bankruptcy and so on – are, in the main, manageable. There is plenty of experience for us all to draw on about these topics and I will cover what I think is the best approach to each as we go along. But the outlook for the period ahead is clouded by the uncertainties of global terrorism and the upheaval in the Middle East.

These are unpleasant circumstances, but I ask you to continue to do what you can to manage your own situation. Many of these global events are out of the control of most of us, and it is very important not to be so overwhelmed by the volatile nature of our world that we forget to focus on the issues where we can make a difference – namely, our own.

Our planet has survived many terrible things, from world wars to disastrous illnesses, such as the bubonic plague which killed millions of people in the fourteenth and seventeenth centuries. Yet humans have shown an amazing resilience and an ability to survive and prosper.

Difficult times will impact on us all at some time or another, and I hope this book helps you to survive when an unfortunate roll of the dice brings an unexpected challenge.

Investing for tough times

Soft landing, bumpy landing, hard landing, crash landing? No, not idle cockpit banter accidentally broadcast over a plane's PA system, but similarly nerve-wracking speculation by economists and other well-credentialed characters about how the economy and investment markets are likely to travel in the months, or even years, ahead. And no wonder the experts are concerned, because everyone else certainly is. Terrorism attacks, the Iraq war and SARS decimating tourism are not highlights of our planet's history, but are real concerns that we face in early 2003. And in the midst of this uncertainty our two favourite assets – property and shares – have performed much like the title of this book.

In 2002 particularly, shares behaved like the snake, while property in our major cities and on many coastal strips saw quite unusual highs – acting more like the ladder. But what about the future? Well, while uncertainty is the only certainty, history remains a powerful guide to the future.

Let's face facts – since the mid-1990s, we were exceptionally lucky to have enjoyed a long period of strong investment returns. And it is great to see that many Australians took advantage of this, and made investing and wealth creation a bigger part of their lives. However, investment markets, like the economy, have always run in cycles. The rise and fall of these markets is perfectly normal, and it is something long-term investors would be familiar with. But in the share market downturn of 2001 and 2002, many share investors were newcomers to the scene who had never experienced a significant fall in investment markets. Understandably, they found these market woes a very unpleasant experience, despite knowing that sooner or later it had to happen, and I didn't enjoy it either.

But, for most of us, wealth creation is a long-term issue. And that makes it something we will have to work on in both good times and bad. Yes, it makes sense to finetune your investment strategy in line with changes in your circumstances, and this book is designed to help you do just that through some of the more challenging times in your life. But, over the long run of, say, seven to ten years, it is likely that you will make investment decisions when things are tough, and when they are not so tough. There will be times when markets are going gangbusters, but there will be other times when they head south. But regardless of how the markets are heading, even during periods when returns are poor, the best way to achieve your long-term goals is by sticking with your long-term strategy. And that can be a real test of an investor's confidence.

Personally, I am not a fan of changing my long-term investment strategy in response to short-term market swings. So many different factors determine what is happening in investment markets that if you want to know how the markets are likely to fare in the short term, you'd do just as well gazing into a tennis ball as you would a crystal ball. No one really knows what the markets are going to do over short periods. So my advice is to forget about these issues (leave them to the economists and politicians) and look beyond them to the longer term, because what I can say with certainty is that mainstream markets never fail over time to recover from a slowdown. And this is something every investor needs to know.

I am very aware that in this new century the old model of starting work at 18, getting married, having children and retiring at age 65 has taken a bit of a beating. We are starting work later, getting into relationships later, divorcing at a higher rate, getting caught up in redundancies and having fewer children (who never leave home!). We are working more hours under greater pressure. Many households have both parents at work. We worry about the quality of our lives, our relationships and our children. But despite the fact that the typical nuclear family of 25 years ago is, for many, just a memory, the old-fashioned rules of financial success are still highly effective. The trick is to understand these rules and how they apply to the global economy we now live in, and to realise that they still apply in both good times and bad. In this chapter I want to look at some of these basic rules and how we can adapt them to our dreams and aspirations.

IT DOESN'T TAKE A LOT TO GET STARTED

Let me make one thing clear upfront. You don't need big amounts of money to be a successful investor. The real trick to investing is to do it regularly, without dipping into your nest egg unless it is absolutely essential, and by that I mean when you really need the money. You might start off with something small, but given time the results can be quite spectacular – especially if you let compounding interest work its magic. The key, though, is to begin *now*. The earlier you start, the sooner compounding returns (where you earn income on your income) can start to do the hard work for you.

Here's a terrific story that illustrates the extent to which returns can mount over the years. In 1626 a fellow named Peter Minuit bought Manhattan Island for the Dutch, paying the native Manhattan Indians just $24 for the entire 20 000 acres. Now, at first glance it would seem the native owners were taken to the cleaners on the deal. However, if they had put their $24 in an investment returning just 6.25% per annum, that initial deposit would have grown to just over $184 *billion* by 2003. That is more than the total assessed value of Manhattan real estate, valued in early 2003 at $169 billion by the New York City Finance Department. Not such a bad exchange after all.

I have to admit there is a catch to the story. The Indians weren't paid in cash. What Minuit actually gave them were beads and trinkets supposedly worth $24. Nonetheless, it's a yarn that certainly shows the power of compounding – particularly over the long term.

Now, I'm certainly not suggesting you need to wait almost 400 years for your investments to amount to anything. But what the story does prove is that you don't have to be a Rockefeller to be a successful investor.

INVEST FOR THE LONG TERM – MARKETS RECOVER

We have always felt comfortable investing in property, and for some time now I've been encouraging ordinary Australians to also invest in shares. That's because investing in growth assets, like shares and property, is a vital part of building your wealth. As Table 1 shows, returns on good quality growth assets, like shares and property, will outpace inflation over time. Without this growth, you face the real prospect of having an investment nest egg with ever-dwindling purchasing power.

But with the good comes the bad. You see, the assets that produce the highest long-term growth often have the greatest short-term fluctuations in value. And sometimes, as Australian and

Table 1: Calendar year market returns January 1983 to December 2002

Year	Australian shares %	International shares %	Australian fixed interest %	Australian listed property %	Cash %
1983	**66.8**	32.2	14.3	50.2	*13.6*
1984	−2.2	**14.4**	12.0	10.1	12.4
1985	44.1	**70.8**	8.1	*5.3*	15.4
1986	**52.2**	45.6	18.9	35.4	*18.1*
1987	−7.9	7.0	**18.6**	5.8	15.3
1988	**17.9**	*4.1*	9.4	16.1	12.8
1989	17.4	**26.2**	14.4	*2.4*	18.4
1990	*−17.5*	−15.1	**19.1**	8.7	16.2
1991	**34.2**	20.0	24.8	20.1	*11.2*
1992	−2.3	4.6	**10.4**	7.0	6.9
1993	**45.4**	24.2	16.3	30.1	*5.4*
1994	−8.7	−8.0	−4.7	−5.6	**5.3**
1995	20.2	**26.1**	18.6	12.7	*8.1*
1996	**14.6**	*6.2*	11.9	14.5	7.6
1997	12.2	**41.6**	12.2	20.3	*5.6*
1998	11.6	**32.3**	9.5	18.0	*5.1*
1999	16.1	**17.2**	−1.2	*−5.0*	5.0
2000	4.8	2.2	12.1	**17.9**	6.3
2001	10.5	*−10.1*	5.5	**15.0**	5.2
2002	−8.6	−27.4	8.8	**11.9**	4.7
Compound Annualised Return	14.1	13.5	11.7	13.9	9.8

Inflation over the period averaged 4.2% p.a.
Bold indicates year's highest return.
Italics indicates year's worst return.
Source: ipac securities.

international shareholders found in 2002, these investments can even take a loss. But when this happens often the best thing to do is sit tight. By holding onto these investments, you let their values recover. The problem is that too many investors bail out at the first whiff of a market downturn.

Consider this: one study, conducted in the 1990s by research group Morningstar, found that managed funds in the United States returned, on average, around 12% per annum in the five years to mid-1994. Yet, over the same period, the average investor in them experienced *losses* of just over 2%. The difference in returns occurred because investors bought into funds when the market, and hence prices, were at a high, but as soon as the market dipped and prices dropped, they sold out.

And if you think about it, when we buy just about anything else, we almost always apply the reverse principle. We buy up big when things are cheap, and sit tight, or sell, when prices are high. It is a philosophy that we should also apply to investing. But all too often we buy shares or property when they are on a market high and at their most expensive, only to panic and sell when prices fall.

But, let me stress again that rises and falls in investment markets are completely normal. They only become a problem if you sell the investment as a knee-jerk reaction to short-term market lows. Not only does this turn a 'paper' loss into a real one, it also makes it more expensive to buy back into the market when values pick up again. And history continually shows us that investment markets recover from slowdowns, sometimes amazingly quickly, with values often going on to greater heights than before. The catch is that no one knows when this upswing is about to happen, which is why sitting tight can be the best option.

A perfect example of the way markets recover after a dip was seen following the terrorist attacks on the United States in September 2001. Not surprisingly, in the immediate aftermath of the crisis, Australian share prices dipped on average by over 6% in just one month. And over the weeks that followed, the market fell in value by about 15%. Even the bluest of blue chip shares were affected, and the prophets of doom who began spouting all sorts of dire predictions started to sound vaguely believable. But here's the catch: the share market recovered with such vigour that by mid-February 2002, the All Ordinaries Index (which measures the changes in value of Australia's largest 500 listed companies) had reached a record high and the doomsayers were being ignored once more.

Over the next year the All Ordinaries fell again, with the uncertainty of the war in Iraq and then the SARS crisis, but the point here is that investment markets have never failed to recover from past shocks, and there is no reason to expect the future will be any different.

That's the good news. The bad news is that following 11 September, plenty of investors, spooked by popular sentiment, sold their shares at a loss. It's an understandable reaction to want to bail out of the markets during times of uncertainty, but shareholders who did nothing more than sit tight through the whole downturn recouped their portfolio values within a remarkably short period of time.

If you take a look at share markets around the world, the same reaction has happened on plenty of other occasions. For example, the stock market crash of October 1987, the start of the Gulf War in 1991 and the Asian economic meltdown of 1997 have all prompted a dip in the value of the All Ordinaries Index. But the market has always recovered.

Wealth creation and management is about having a sensible strategy and sticking to it. Certainly your strategy should be adapted to the conditions, but it is important to stick to your plans.

DON'T TRY TO 'TIME' THE MARKET

Trying to pick the market cycle and sell at the highs and buy at the lows sounds great, but it is nonsense – you just won't get it right consistently.

No one can say just when markets are about to head south – nor will you know when the market is set to rise. There are armies of professionals with their fingers on the market pulse who devote their working lives to timing the market. And they don't always get it right. In fact, they get it wrong quite often. Sure, I'd prefer to buy at the absolute bottom of the market, but who knows when that is? It could be today – or in two years. And that's why successful investors know that time in the market, in other words, sticking with your investments for the long term, is more important than market timing.

You probably won't always get the timing right, and there may be times in the short term when you may wish you had waited. But over time your investments should weather both the ups and the downs and, as you'll see in the next section, you are better off making the decision to invest than making no decision at all.

THE WORST STRATEGY OF ALL

If one of the worst things you can do is to join the stampede to sell your investments during a downturn, 'failing to invest at all' heads the list of investment disasters.

People put off investing for all sorts of reasons. But putting it off because you are waiting for the market to pick up is a mug's game, and a guaranteed recipe for disaster. To show you just how much *not* investing will cost you, let's imagine four investors, each of whom had $1000 to invest about 19 years ago, in mid-1984.

Our hypothetical Investor A has been exceptionally lucky and every year invested in the market that paid the highest returns for the year. Investor B has had really bad luck and picked the worst-performing market each year. Investor C took an each-way bet and divided the initial sum equally across most mainstream investment markets. Investor D was convinced that better returns and lower share and property prices (and hence better investment opportunities) were just around the corner, and so never quite got around to investing at all. The table below shows the value of their portfolios, some 19 years later, in July 2002.

Approximate value of $1000 invested since July 1984*

Investor A – best returns each year	Investor B – worst returns each year	Investor C – earns average return of all asset classes	Investor D – never gets around to investing
$91 000	$1300	$14 500	$1000

*Based on ipac securities' financial year market returns from 1 July 1984 to 30 June 2002.

Naturally, the best results go to Investor A, who picked the highest-yielding markets for each year, and as you'd expect, Investor C did quite well. But surprisingly, Investor B, who copped the worst returns every year for almost two decades, still earned almost $300 more than Investor D, who did nothing. In other words, despite selecting the flops of each year – plenty of which dished up negative returns – Investor B still made money.

The odds of consistently picking the best performing market, year after year, are pretty slim – probably about equal to picking the Melbourne Cup trifecta each year for a decade. Thankfully, though, it's equally unlikely that you would pick the worst performing investment every year. But, what is easily achievable is earning a return that is somewhere between the highest and lowest returns, and that is exactly what Investor C has done.

Look, there are plenty of so-called experts out there who talk about the 'best' time to invest and 'market timing', but the fact remains that the time to start investing is *now*. Every day that you put off investing is a day when you could have been building your wealth. You will do better by putting your money in an investment today that earns 5% over the next 12 months, for example, than you will if you wait six months to get a 9% return (which is much harder to achieve) for the rest of the year. The strategy that will leave you with the leanest wallet over the long term is not investing at all.

WHAT SHOULD I INVEST IN?

People often ask me what the 'best' investment is. I tell them that investing is very much a case of horses for courses and there's no single investment that is 'best' for everybody. Having said that, the one rule that holds true for everyone is that you can only expect to get higher returns from an investment if you're prepared to take on more risk. And while we all want high returns, not all of us are comfortable with a high degree of risk.

This idea of risk and return is important because, very broadly speaking, investments can be classified as either 'income' (also known as 'conservative') assets, or 'growth' assets. Income assets are so-called because their return is generally in the form of fairly regular, predictable income, while growth assets are so-named because in addition to an ongoing return, you also get some capital growth. But while growth assets offer the potential for decent long-term returns, they also have more risk. Determining the investment strategy that is best for you really does call for some help from a professional financial adviser. A good course of action would be to have a look below at the main types of assets before you speak to a financial adviser, so that you have an understanding of the basics. Then, maybe come back and take another look at them so that the advice you are being given makes sense to you.

Income assets

Income or conservative assets include things like term deposits, cash management trusts and other interest-bearing securities. These generally pay investors a specified income on a regular basis. This lets you budget more easily, and because they are low risk you are less likely to lose any sleep over them. However, there are some downsides to these investments. Firstly, the returns are unlikely to set your pulse racing. The calendar year market returns 1983–2002 on page 5 show that the 20-year annualised return from cash was 9.8% compared to, say, 14.1% for Australian shares.

The return for cash is lower because this tends to be a very secure investment. But there are two other issues that you need to weigh up with this asset class, and the first is tax. The income on interest-bearing investments like a term deposit is fully taxable. For example, if you are on the top marginal rate of tax of 48.5%, a return of 4% on a savings deposit will be reduced to almost 2% once the taxman has taken his cut.

The second concern is that income assets don't give you much opportunity for capital growth. And this is a serious issue when you are talking about long-term investing. You see, over long periods of time, inflation will eat away at the value of an asset unless it grows in value faster than inflation.

To give you an idea of how you need to protect your wealth from the ravages of inflation, consider this: a haircut that costs you $15 today is likely to cost around $35 in twenty years' time (assuming inflation hovers around the average for the last 20 years of 4.2%). A Sunday newspaper will cost around $3.50, and a pair of shoes costing $50 today will set you back about $113 twenty years down the track. And unless you have at least part of your portfolio invested in growth-type investments whose value will keep up with the level of inflation over time, these everyday items could begin to look like luxuries.

Now, that is not to say that income assets are not worth having – far from it. They certainly have a place in every portfolio for the security and reliability of income they offer. What you need to consider is how *much* of your money you should invest in this type of asset, and again this is where the advice of a competent professional financial adviser can play an important role.

Growth assets

Growth assets include shares (both international and Australian) and property, as well as units in managed funds that invest in both of these. These investments offer ongoing income from dividends, rent and distributions (all of which can have tax breaks), but they also offer capital growth. It is important to remember, however, that these investments have more risk and the capital growth is by no means guaranteed. There can be periods when the markets for these investments go gangbusters (often called a 'bull' market) and there will also be periods when the markets dip (a 'bear' market).

And while it's great to watch the value of your investment climb – daily, in some cases, if you are talking about shares – you also need to be able to withstand a fall in the value of your investment, which is definitely not as much fun.

Regardless of the type of assets you invest in, your best defence against market downturns is to have a well-diversified portfolio of quality mainstream investments combined with the discipline to resist selling out during periods of poor or even negative returns.

DIVERSITY

Diversity is about *not* putting all your eggs in one basket. Take another look at the example I gave on page 9 of the four investors who each invested in the best-performing markets, the worst-performing markets, the average-returning markets and not investing at all. I pointed out that achieving the best or worst investments in each and every year over about two decades is not easy, but what most of us can do consistently is get a near-average return. And, as the results of that example showed, the way to do this is by spreading your money across a range of investments.

Relying on one type of investment is a bit like gambling with your wealth – you could pick the best-performing asset, but you could just as easily pick the dog every time.

DOLLAR COST AVERAGING

In addition to diversifying, another way to maximise your returns while lowering your risk is 'dollar cost averaging'. This is where you invest the same amount on a regular basis, no matter what investment markets are doing. All you have to do is decide how much and how often you are going to invest. You may decide to invest, say, $500 in the share market, on a monthly, six-monthly or yearly basis – it doesn't really matter, as long as you stick with it. This way you will tend to buy the *least* when the market is expensive and *more* when the market is cheap, so you average out the cost of your investments, rather than worrying about getting your market timing right.

I am a big fan of dollar cost averaging because it's so easy and it gets you into a disciplined investment regimen. The averaging process ultimately means you might not get any bargains, but you shouldn't pay too much for your investments either. You simply keep adding to your portfolio come rain, hail or shine.

WE ALL HAVE THE ABILITY TO GET RICH – SLOWLY

No investment will give you instant wealth and you should be extremely wary of anything or anyone who claims to know how to do just that. Very few of us will get rich quickly. Wealth comes over time by building up assets and generally behaving in a logical fashion. Booms and busts are a natural part of the economic cycle and, despite the best hopes of Reserve Banks around the world, our chances of managing the economy into a perpetual growth pattern are somewhere between nil and none.

So if, like me, you reckon your best chance of creating wealth is by planning to do so over two or more decades, then you may as well get used to the economic realities of life that have been hidden due to the very extensive economic boom of the last ten years.

Markets may change over time, but your portfolio should reflect where *you* are with regard to your age, your level of comfort with risk and your future goals – both short term and long term. Follow a long-term investment plan and stick with it, rather than looking at where the market currently is. The market will always be different a few months or a few years down the track but in the long term, history has shown us that markets move forward and produce good returns.

The last two decades have seen all sorts of revolutions in the Australian lifestyle: more of us are studying; more of us work in so-called 'white-collar' jobs; we are retiring younger and a whole lot more is changing in between. A revolution has also taken place in our financial lives, in the way we think about, and take responsibility for, our own financial wellbeing. We have come to realise that the government cannot look after all of us in our retirement and that *we* are the ones who are responsible for our own and our family's future.

Tough times will come and go, investment markets will have highs and lows, but we need to make plans for our future – and we need to put them into action and stick with them. Without these plans, and the discipline to follow them, our dreams of wealth and financial independence will remain just that.

Investment strategies for tough times

- Unless you need the money, why change your long-term investments if your long-term strategy hasn't changed?
- Different investment markets rarely move in the same direction at the same time. So instead of trying to pick the best-performing investment each year, diversify across a range of assets. It will cushion your losses if one market dips, and increase your chances of being invested in those sectors of the market that prosper.

Student days

At age 18, with a dozen consecutive years of schooling under your belt, the thought of undertaking more study may seem pretty unappealing. But I reckon one of the best financial decisions you can ever make is to get tertiary qualifications. Whether it's a course at a TAFE (Technical and Further Education) college, a private college or a university degree, you'll be giving yourself a head start that lasts a lifetime.

That's not to say it's easy, though. In addition to the challenges posed by assignments and exams, many students face the added hurdle of surviving on a shoestring budget. This chapter looks at ways of stretching your money a bit further during these financially lean years in your life, but even when times get tough, the important thing is to keep going and complete your studies (which I urge you to do), because most graduates agree the hardship was well worth it.

Sure, tertiary study means putting off your first real pay cheque for a while longer, but research shows that just a few years after graduation, you are likely to be well ahead of your friends who opted to join the workforce at age 18.

HIGHER EDUCATION DEFINITELY PAYS

The grand traditions of student life often include earning a meagre wage, possibly in a dead-end job, spending at least as much as you earn at the local pub, with the concept of making strides with your personal finances being about as alien as missing 'Happy Hour' at the student bar. But the main reason students continue to line up for this lifestyle is because they know they are making a short-term investment in their long-term prospects.

And, according to a study* by the National Centre for Economic and Social Modelling (NATSEM), higher education definitely does pay. A uni graduate can expect to be in full-time work from the age of 21 (after completing their degree) to the age of 63, with their income rising each year up to around the age of 53. A secondary school leaver, on the other hand, can expect around four years of unemployment during their working life, and will enjoy an annual increase in income only up to age 42, after which it will start to decline.

The same study showed that the years of financial sacrifice at university are quickly compensated for. A graduate, by age 21, can earn an annual income of around $37 000, compared to about $26 000 for the school leaver. And if that doesn't convince you, NATSEM also reckons that over the course of a lifetime, a university graduate will earn total income of just under $3 million, which is almost 60% more than the school leaver, who can expect a life-long income of about $1.8 million. And that's despite graduates starting work later.

* P. Johnson & R. Lloyd, 'Does Higher Education Pay? Results from the Returns to Education Model', National Centre for Economic and Social Modelling, University of Canberra, July 2000.

The rosier outlook for graduates even continues into retirement. The better-paid graduate is likely to have contributed more to super during his or her working life, and so can expect to be better off in retirement also.

These projections are not based on graduates with one of the high-paying degrees, like law or medicine, tucked under their belts. The NATSEM figures were based on a three-year science degree. But there's no doubt *any* tertiary qualification makes you more employable.

Having said that, not all tertiary qualifications produce the same results. As you would expect, some pay more handsomely than others. Your dentist may not be the most popular person you'll ever visit, but they are likely to be one of the wealthiest, with graduates in this field consistently enjoying the top starting salary of around $46 000 in 2001. This compares to the average starting salary for a new graduate of around $35 000, which is certainly nothing to be sniffed at.

If you're considering a TAFE course rather than a university degree, the job prospects together with an indication of average earnings for just about every occupation imaginable are listed on the web site of the Department of Employment and Workplace Relations at www.jobsearch.gov.au.

Incomes aside, though, graduates of both TAFE and university can look forward to better career opportunities, and the reason for this doesn't just lie in their chosen field of study. The real value of education is that it trains you to think, to question and to find solutions to problems, and by completing some form of tertiary education you achieve something tangible and have a document to prove it. Not only does this boost your self-esteem, confidence and skills, it demonstrates to an employer that you have the grit and ability to see something you've started through to a successful end. And that's a quality all employers value and seek.

It's not the end of the world if you end up in a field of work unrelated to your area of study. My own undergraduate degree (a Bachelor of Arts) had little to do with money management, but the range of learning experiences I enjoyed, from part-time work to involvement in various university clubs, proved to be a strong foundation in building the skills needed to start my own business.

That's the good news. The downside to being a student is the cost. In addition to annual college or university fees, you may also be up for the Higher Education Contribution Scheme (HECS). Students living away from home have to consider accommodation costs and, of course, there are textbooks to buy. However, all these expenses should be looked on as an *investment in your future* with your additional qualifications being a ticket to a better-paid job. The odds are that you'll reap the benefits of the investment you've made in yourself many times over. In that light then, assuming you've got the opportunity to undertake study, I firmly believe you'd be absolutely crazy not to. But meeting the financial challenges of student life is no mean feat. So, what are the costs, and how do you best manage them?

HIGHER EDUCATION CONTRIBUTION SCHEME (HECS)

The idea behind HECS is that students should contribute to the cost of their tertiary education. It's a Commonwealth Government levy applied to university courses, but there can be exceptions. For example, HECS isn't charged if your course is fully funded by an employer.

In most cases, HECS is based on the units of study you undertake, rather than your overall degree. Areas of study are classified into three categories or 'bands', each with a separate HECS cost. The higher-paying subjects like law and medicine are in the most expensive band (Band 3). The middle band includes subjects like business and engineering, while most of the arts-based subjects, including education, are in the least expensive band

(Band 1). The full table of HECS bands appears at the end of this chapter, however the cost of each band is updated annually in line with inflation and revised amounts can be seen on the HECS web site at www.hecs.gov.au.

The costs per band are for each full-time, full year of study. For example, if you want to undertake a Bachelor of Arts degree, you'll generally need to complete the equivalent of three years of full-time study. At 2003 rates, this will leave you with a total HECS debt in the order of $11 040 (being $3680 per year for each of the three years). If you want to add a few Band 2 subjects like, say, economics, you can expect to pay more.

As HECS is based on your study load, it will vary according to the number of units you undertake – the fewer units you study in a year, the less HECS you pay. It is charged on a semester basis (there are two semesters in the academic year), and your university will calculate your HECS contribution for you at the start of each semester, based on the subjects you have chosen. At this stage the figure is only an estimate, as students often change their study load in the first few weeks of the semester.

There are several payment options that can make your HECS burden a bit lighter. One option is to defer paying HECS until you are in the workforce. Once your income exceeds the repayment threshold, currently set at $24 365 (indexed annually to match average earnings), you are required to contribute 3% of your income to repaying HECS. This contribution rises to the top rate of 6% once you earn over $43 859. When you start work, you need to let your employer know that you have an outstanding HECS debt, as they are obliged to start withholding additional amounts to cover HECS repayments once you earn over $463 each week.

It is worth noting that when it comes to HECS, the income on which your debt is repaid is calculated in a slightly different way than it is for income tax. Your HECS income is taken to be your taxable income (which includes the usual things like salary, interest income and so on), *plus* any losses you have claimed on a rental property, *plus* any taxable fringe benefits. I realise that the majority of students just entering the workforce may not have property investments, although it may certainly apply to mature-age students, but some will have received fringe benefits, like the provision of a car. These amounts need to be taken into account when you are letting your employer know you have an outstanding HECS debt.

If you never earn over the payment threshold of $24 365, you never repay anything. And it is estimated that around 17% of total HECS debts will never be repaid, either because the ex-students don't enter the workforce or because their income never goes over the threshold. You won't be charged interest on the outstanding debt, but the balance is adjusted each year for inflation.

Most people who choose to defer their HECS debt take around six years to pay it off. Once the debt is repaid, you need to let your employer know, so that the amount of tax withheld from your wage or salary can be reduced.

Another way to trim back your HECS debt, if you have the funds to do it, is to pay each semester's HECS charge upfront and get a 25% 'discount'. Let's say, for example, that your university advises you that your HECS debt for semester one is $1800. If you pay your HECS upfront, taking the 25% discount into account, you will pay a total of $1350.

A question that often comes up is whether or not it is better to defer paying HECS and invest the money (if you have it) in something else. My answer is that you are probably better off paying upfront. A 25% discount is a pretty substantial one, and remember that your HECS debt will increase with inflation, but the value of your investment may not. I mentioned earlier that a surprisingly large proportion of HECS is never paid off, and certainly if you are doing a degree just out of interest, or if you don't expect to earn over the HECS income threshold, it may not make sense to pay upfront and get the discount. But, for most people, the whole point of studying for a degree is to get a decent, well-paying job, in which case it is generally worth considering making an upfront payment.

If you don't have the money to pay early, it is still worth paying at least $500 or more of the outstanding amount, as this gets you a bonus of 15% on the amount you pay. For example, you only need to pay $600 to have your HECS bill reduced by $690. You can find out the balance of your HECS debt at any time by contacting the Australian Tax Office on 132 861.

> If you plan to make voluntary payments on your HECS debt, make sure you pay before 1 June each year, as this is when the outstanding debt is adjusted (upwards, of course) for inflation.

OTHER EDUCATIONAL EXPENSES

Whether you attend a university, TAFE college or another private college, you will be hit with a variety of campus-related fees. 'Student union' fees are paid annually and vary between institutions, ranging from less than $100 to a few hundred each year. TAFE courses tend to be far cheaper – to begin with, you won't pay HECS. The cost of a diploma in the New South Wales TAFE system, for example, was just $690 in 2002.

If you have difficulties scraping enough together for student fees, it is worth approaching your student council about the possibility of deferring the cost, organising a schedule of payments, or taking out a student loan (more on this later). The main point I want to make here, though, is that completing your education and getting those additional qualifications should be your main priority.

Some students start out at TAFE and transfer to university, getting accreditation on the way for the TAFE subjects they have studied. On one hand this can trim your HECS bill, but the downside is that it can extend the amount of time you spend as a student. Only around 2% of students choose this option, but it has been enough to attract the attention of our policy makers who have raised the prospect of a HECS-style fee for students who move from TAFE to university.

> If you are enrolled in a broad area of study, you will enhance your job prospects if you include some more specialised subjects in your course.

Textbooks

Textbooks don't come cheap and with several books often required for each semester, they can certainly blow a hole in your budget. They are a necessity, though, and the good news is that most colleges and universities have second-hand book exchanges where you can try to recoup some of the cost when you have finished with them.

Also, most campuses run a 'co-operative' bookshop where students pay a few dollars to become a member and are then entitled to a 5–10% discount off the list price of new books. When you complete your course, you can cease being a member and your initial joining fee is refunded.

Educational Textbook Subsidy Scheme (ETSS) Introduced in July 2000, this scheme is designed to give students relief from the GST impost on textbooks. Here's how it works. Students approach a bookshop with a copy of their prescribed text or recommended reading list. The bookseller gives the student a discount for GST (capped at 8% of the retail purchase price), and then claims the subsidy back from the Commonwealth Department of Education, Science and Training (DEST), which administers the scheme.

Not all book retailers are involved in the scheme, so you should look for a bookshop displaying the ETSS shopfront logo. In addition, it's important to make sure the book you are after is on a list provided by your lecturer, otherwise you may not get the discount.

Accommodation

Unless you choose to live at home during your student years, the cost of HECS, fees and even books could pale into insignificance compared to the cost of accommodation. Students can choose from a range of options, from fully catered residential colleges located on or near campus, right through to renting a flat or house with other students. The cost can vary enormously. At the budget end of the spectrum, it's possible to get by on next to nothing if you are prepared to cram in with half a dozen other desperate students and you don't mind being last in line for the shower. Or, you can spend more and get the deluxe option of fully catered on-campus lodgings.

Homestay This is where students live with another family in the vicinity of their campus. Student newsletters or notice boards are a good source of advertisements for this type of accommodation, which can be a cheap option. On the downside, it is often hard moving in with people you barely know, and it is probably not the best alternative if you are living away from home for the first time.

On-campus colleges The weekly cost of campus colleges or 'halls of residence' as they are also known varies from around $70 (with no meals) to $160 (all meals provided), depending on the facilities. Most include a private bedroom with a study desk, but other facilities are generally shared. Catered colleges may seem expensive at first glance, but the overall cost is not too bad when you consider you don't have to provide furniture, you won't have to pay rental over holiday periods, and for first-year students in particular, it reduces the culture shock of going from a home environment to independent living.

Just as important as the cost is whether or not you are suited to college living. Some students thrive in the lifestyle, others don't. It all depends on your personality and what you are hoping to get out of your experience as a student. Personally, I found my three years at Baxter College, an on-campus college at the University of NSW, to be a marvellous experience.

Off-campus share accommodation If you are considering share accommodation, regional universities offer cheaper rentals than metropolitan areas. The downside to this, though, is the possibility of fewer job opportunities. A survey by the Department of Family and Community Services (FACS) has Sydney ranked as our most expensive city in which to live, where a two-bedroom flat costs around $270 a week. Perth, Adelaide and Hobart rank as our cheapest capital cities, where, for a similar property, you will pay about half that amount.

Most residential leases run for six to 12 months, and you will need to budget for quite a few upfront costs well before you move in. You will be asked to pay a rental bond of four weeks' rent (it can be six weeks for a furnished property) plus the first month's rent in advance. On top of this, you may need to pay for telephone, electricity and, possibly, gas connections. As a tenant, you do not pay water rates, but you can be asked to pay for the water you use (this is set out on the landlord's rate notice). You will need at least the bare essentials of furniture and, if you have any valuables such as a stereo or a computer, you may want to take out home contents insurance.

Whichever option your budget extends to, it's a good idea to get your living arrangements sorted out early. Accommodation around many colleges and universities becomes scarce once the semester begins.

Let your bank or credit union know that you are a student. Many will waive monthly account-keeping fees or point you in the direction of a low-fee student account, which can mean a monthly saving of up to $15. Like the rest of us, though, you will still be slugged with a charge of up to $1.50 if you use another bank's ATM.

WHERE TO STUDY

Just as different jobs offer better pay, some educational institutions have better results in terms of their employment record and even the rates of pay you can expect as a new graduate. The Department of Education, Science and Training (DEST) publishes the annual employment rates and starting salaries for graduates from almost all Australian universities. You'll find it on their web site at www.dest.gov.au. Happily, there is reasonably little variation between the employment success rates of different universities, and around 81% of all graduates find full-time employment shortly after leaving university, with an average starting salary (across all disciplines) of about $35 000 for the year 2001.

You also need to weigh up a few other considerations when you are deciding where to study. Things like the part-time job opportunities in the region (noting that they are generally better in metropolitan areas) might be an issue for you. But you should also look at the potential for new experiences. For a city-based school leaver, studying at a regional university or college can bring experiences that are as valuable to employers as your qualifications.

These days all educational institutions, both public and private, compete for students and the funding they bring. You will be investing a considerable amount of time and money into the place and the course you will be studying, so, like any investment, it is worth checking out its credentials before you commit to it. Some institutions may claim their courses are approved by professional organisations when they are not, others claim to have resources which may not exist, and others boast of 100% employment success rates.

In addition, DEST has issued a warning about organisations that call themselves universities or colleges while not being accredited by the government at all. A growing phenomenon, these bogus providers (often called 'degree mills') offer degrees involving little or no study. It might sound like a good idea (especially if you are still recovering from six consecutive years of high school), but they are definitely something to be avoided. Only higher education providers listed with the Australian Qualification Framework (AQF) are recognised by the Commonwealth, state and territory governments. So it's not a bad idea to look up the AQF web site (www.aqf.edu.au/accred.htm) or give them a call on 03 9639 1606, to see if your planned place of study is accredited.

For my money, one of the best ways to find out how well your place and course of study is regarded in the workforce is to speak to employers within your field of study. It also helps to keep an eye on the employment section of the newspapers to make sure that the skills and qualifications you are working towards are getting mentioned in job vacancy ads.

PAYING FOR IT ALL

The majority of students, around 70%, undertake their studies full-time. For many of these students, money can be tight. Paid employment is an important source of income for most, but around a quarter of students receive government support.

It is worth putting the money situation in perspective, though. Students traditionally have pretty moderate financial needs (take note that I'm talking about 'needs' as distinct from 'wants'). When I look back on my own years at university, I'm amazed at how little money I survived on. I spent two nights a week pulling beers at a local pub for the grand wage of $33. It doesn't sound like much now (it wasn't much then!), but in those days it seemed that I always had some cash in my pocket. My only possessions were jeans and T-shirts and a $120 pushbike – none of which generated too many bills. I didn't have a family to support or a mortgage to pay off, so even though it sounds like I lived on a pittance, my financial needs were pretty modest.

It's the same for students today. By putting off big financial commitments and steering clear of debt-inducing credit cards, students can focus on investing in their own education. Nonetheless, since student life involves getting by on a minimum, it is important to be organised when it comes to money and that means using a budget. You'll find a Budget Planner at the end of this book, and for students on any income, the time taken to complete it is a good investment in keeping your head above water, and not bad practice for when you begin to earn a more robust income.

GOVERNMENT SUPPORT

Youth Allowance and Austudy are the main sources of government support for tertiary students. If you are eligible, you can expect to receive somewhere between $5000 and $6000 per annum. It will help keep the wolf from the door, but it certainly won't see you mixing it with the champagne and caviar set – more the sardines and spumante scene.

Youth Allowance
Youth Allowance is paid to full-time students aged 16 to 24 and part-time students aged up to 21. The current payment for a student

living away from home is about $300 a fortnight, but the rates are adjusted quarterly to reflect changes in the cost of living.

Students don't automatically receive the allowance. It is subject to a parental income test, and is reduced if your parents' income is over $27 400 (more if you have other dependent siblings). If mum and dad earn over the threshold, students will need to prove their independence. This is not so easy for the average 18-year-old, because for Centrelink purposes, you are independent only if:

- you have been out of school for 18 months and have earned over about $15 400, or
- you have been working at least 18 months to support yourself, or
- you have been married or in a de facto relationship for at least 12 months.

Even if you meet these conditions, the allowance is subject to a personal income test. The income limits are set out at the end of the chapter, but most students can earn around $236 each fortnight before their allowance is reduced.

Students aged 16 to 24 who live away from home may also be eligible for rent assistance of about $90 per fortnight.

Austudy

Austudy provides income support for full-time students aged over 25. The payment rates are similar to Youth Allowance and again, students can earn around $236 each fortnight before their payment is reduced. There is no parental means test for Austudy, as Centrelink regards 25-year-old students as being independent, and no rental assistance is available.

Abstudy

Abstudy is paid to Indigenous students and the rates and terms of payment are similar to Youth Allowance.

Income bank

If students receiving Youth Allowance, Austudy and Abstudy earn less than $236 per fortnight, Centrelink records the difference as a credit in what is called its 'income bank'. During periods of, say, the summer holidays when most students take on part-time jobs, their income tends to increase. When this happens, Centrelink uses up the credits in the student's income bank rather than cutting back their study payment.

Let's say, for example, that Liz, a full-time student in receipt of Austudy, earns $50 one fortnight from her part-time job. When this happens a credit of $186 ($236 less $50) will be recorded as a credit in her income bank. The next fortnight Liz earns $350 from her job, which is $114 over the income limit of $236. Instead of reducing her payment, Centrelink deduct the $114 from her income bank, leaving her with a balance of $72 ($186 less $114). It simply saves her having a full Austudy payment one week and virtually none the next. The maximum balance you can have in the income bank is $6000.

Other benefits

Additional benefits available to students receiving Youth Allowance, Austudy or Abstudy include a fare allowance for travel between your place of education and home; a health care card; a pharmaceutical allowance; an interest-free advance of up to $500; as well as the ability to access the Student Financial Supplement Scheme, which we look at on page 32.

SCHOLARSHIPS

Scholarships are amounts awarded by various organisations to help students pay their way through their education. The amounts involved can range from a few hundred dollars to a few thousand. However, in terms of their value to your job prospects, they are worth a lot more than just the income they provide.

Scholarships are definitely a drawcard for employers looking for the top graduates. An added sweetener is that the money is exempt from income tax as long as the scholarship doesn't tie you to a particular employer.

Scholarships are not always awarded on the basis of academic results. They can be granted on the basis of talent in a particular field, or for students with a disability or from a certain ethnic background. What is common to all scholarships, though, is that they are hotly contested. You should start looking into them midway through the year *before* you start your studies, as some applications close in September.

Individual universities offer their own scholarships, but the Department of Education, Science and Training (DEST) have an extensive list of scholarships on their web site at www.dest. gov.au/highered/scholarships.htm.

PART-TIME WORK

Most tertiary students are not too fussy about the type of part-time work they can get, often seeing it as a means to an end. However, part-time jobs have benefits that go way beyond paying for textbooks and a few drinks at the student bar. Experience in even the most mundane jobs will tell future employers that you can handle the combined demands of study and work, and a lack of work experience leaves a big hole in your resume.

If you can get part-time work in the area of your chosen career so much the better, as it will stand you in good stead when you start looking for a full-time position. A number of large corporations offer summer holiday 'cadetships', which not only provide extensive training and are often well paid, but which can be a gateway to a full-time position on graduation. Like scholarships, though, competition for these is intense, so again, apply early.

That said, any job – no matter how unrelated to your future

career – will increase your skill base, and the bonus is that you get paid. The key, however, is to keep a balance. Don't let your academic results suffer because you're overdoing it at work.

Most TAFEs and universities have their own careers centres, and the Graduate Careers Council of Australia web site, which features a job vacancy search, can be found at www.gradlink.edu.au. If you can't get a part-time job in your prospective field and you want to try volunteer work to get relevant experience, the web site for Australian Volunteers International is located at www. ozvol.org.au.

Army Reserve

Cash-strapped tertiary students are less likely to question this option than many of us. The pay, which starts at $53 a day, is tax-free, so it won't affect the tax you pay on any other income. As a member of the Army Reserve, you will need to complete an annual two-week training block, plus one weekend a month. Navy and Air Force reservists will need to complete 32 days each year. The Army Reserve can be contacted on 131 901. Their web address is www.army.gov.au.

OTHER SOURCES OF FUNDS

Student loans

If you are really struggling for cash, it is worth approaching your student union or the university or college administration to apply for a student loan. Generally speaking, the amount of money lent to students is small, ranging from a few hundred dollars to be repaid in two or three months, to around $1500 to be repaid before you graduate. These loans are usually only made to students who are making good academic progress and competition for them can be intense. However, if you are looking for low-cost funds, make this your first port of call as it is likely to be the cheapest option.

Student Financial Supplement Scheme (SFSS)

This loan scheme allows students to exchange their Centrelink payments (Youth Allowance, Austudy or Abstudy) in return for a loan. For every $1 you give up in Centrelink payments, you receive $2 of borrowings. For example, instead of receiving $3000 worth of Austudy, you can opt to receive a $6000 loan. The loans generally range from $500 to $7000.

No credit checks are required to get a loan, and you won't need a guarantor (someone who guarantees to take over the debt if you cannot repay it). The big advantage of these loans over, say, a personal loan from a bank or credit union, is that you don't pay interest (although the outstanding balance is adjusted for changes to inflation). The funds ultimately come from the Commonwealth Bank, but the Federal Government picks up the interest tab. You must start paying it off after five years if your taxable income reaches the current threshold of $32 918. The repayments are based on a percentage of your income, starting at 2% and capped at 4% once you earn around $52 000.

Any voluntary repayments of the student loan are given an increased value. For example, a repayment of $850 will reduce the balance of the loan by $1000, so to repay the loan in full, you need only pay 85% of the total amount outstanding.

At first glance, these loans may sound like a good deal, but the catch is that you can find yourself paying off a big amount for only a small increase in your income. Let's say, for example, that you are entitled to an annual Youth Allowance of $6000, but with some big expenses coming up, you know you will need $8000 to get through the year. So you only need $2000 more, but in order to get the additional funds through SFSS, you will need to trade in $2000 worth of ongoing income for a $4000 loan. This will reduce your income to $4000 (remember for every $1 you give up you get a loan of $2). So, what you are doing is taking out a loan of $4000 (and you will repay more because it is indexed for inflation) to increase your overall income by $2000, which doesn't make great financial sense.

There is no doubt that emergencies sometimes occur sending the best laid financial plans awry, but, as I've already mentioned, if you need emergency funds it may be best to approach your student union first. You may end up paying some interest on loans from these sources, but at least you won't be required to repay money that would have otherwise been paid to you as income.

Commercial student loans

These loans are marketed under a variety of names, including 'campus' loans and 'deferred payment' loans. They are offered by some of our major banks and usually come as part of a tertiary student financial package, often including account fee concessions and a credit card option.

The loans themselves form the core of the package and they are quite different to standard personal loans. For one thing, there's often no loan establishment fee and the interest rates are usually slightly lower than for unsecured personal loans. The real draw-card for students, however, is that you usually don't have to make any repayments until after you graduate. In some cases, repayment can be deferred for up to five years.

And we are not talking small amounts. Graduate loans range in size from a few thousand dollars to around $40 000 in some cases. What's more, they are often remarkably easy to obtain. Some banks will run a credit assessment of applicants, but a guarantor may only be required in limited circumstances – for example, where a student has a poor academic record and no part-time job.

I am a huge believer in investing in your own education, and if it comes down to taking out one of these loans or not completing your studies, I certainly recommend you go for the loan. But – and it's a big but – these loans are to be used with caution. Not only are they relatively easy to get hold of, but the amount you owe also builds up without any effort. That's because the repayments may be delayed, but the interest is not. Interest accrues from the day you draw on the money, so the outstanding balance can swell considerably by the time the first repayment is due. And in some cases, the interest jumps to the standard personal loan rate once you have graduated.

Let's say that a student uses one of these loans to borrow $5000 at the (March 2003) rate of 10.95%. By the time the loan is due for repayment five years later, the accruing interest will have blown out the principal to around $8400 – an increase of almost 70%. Add to this an outstanding HECS debt and you can see why some students leave university with a degree in one hand and debt statements to the value of $20 000 or more in the other.

If you must use one of these loans, be sure to borrow only what you need to cover fees, textbooks and the like, and as soon as you start full-time work, make repayment of the loan a priority. Like any debt, a small lump sum payment can greatly reduce your total interest bill, so it's a good idea to put any tax refunds towards repaying the loan, even when you are still studying. And as for those credit cards that come with the student loan package – give them a miss. They are too much of a temptation for cash-hungry students.

INVESTMENT TIPS FOR STUDENTS

Do

- regard the time you spend in further education as an investment in the best asset you will ever have – your own ability to generate a good income!
- complete any courses that you believe will enhance your skills – anything from public speaking to a Securities Institute course
- learn to manage credit

- travel if you get the chance – it's an education in itself
- work part-time, preferably in a job that will give you course-related experience
- start to think about your short-term, medium-term and long-term financial goals.

Don't

- borrow heavily for items such as a sound system or clothes. Save up to pay in cash and haggle over the price
- have several credit cards
- blow too much money on things that lose their value quickly (cars are a classic culprit in this category)
- worry too much at this stage about long-term investments like super – these will work better for you when your student days are over and you are earning a full-time income.

Useful web sites

Careers information	www.myfuture.edu.au
Centrelink	www.centrelink.gov.au
Commonwealth Government Youth Portal	www.youth.gov.au
Department of Education, Science and Training	www.dest.gov.au
Graduate Careers Council of Australia	www.gradlink.edu.au

HECS cost per band of study

Band	Type of unit	HECS cost per unit – 2003
Band 1	Arts, humanities, social studies, behavioural sciences, education, visual and performing arts, nursing, justice and legal studies	$3680
Band 2	Computing, other health sciences, agriculture, architecture, sciences, administration, business, economics, engineering, maths	$5242
Band 3	Medicine, law, veterinary science, dentistry and dental services	$6136

Source: www.hecs.gov.au, 2003.

Youth Allowance rates

Family situation	Payment per fortnight (indexed)
Single, no children, aged under 18, living at home	$169.70
Single, no children, aged under 18, living away from home	$310.10
Single, aged 18 and over, living away from home	$310.10
Single, aged 18 and over, living at home	$204.20
Single, with children	$406.40
Partnered, no children	$310.10
Partnered, with children	$340.60

Source: Centrelink, as at March 2003.

Austudy rates

Family situation	Payment per fortnight (indexed)
Single	$310.10
Single, with children	$406.40
Partnered, with children	$340.60
Partnered, no children	$310.10

Source: Centrelink, as at March 2003.

Income test – Youth Allowance and Austudy

Family situation	Income allowed (per fortnight) for full payment (indexed)	Income allowed (per fortnight) for part payment (indexed)
Single, aged under 18, living at home	Up to $236	Less than $501.29
Single, aged 18 or over, living at home	Up to $236	Less than $550.57
Single or partnered, living away from home	Up to $236	Less than $701.86
Partnered, with dependants	Up to $236	Less than $745.43
Single, with dependants	Up to $236	Less than $839.43
Long-term unemployed aged 21 or over, entering full-time study and living at home	Up to $236	Less than $617.00
Partnered students, with no children	Up to $236	Less than $745.43

Source: Centrelink, as at March 2003.

Funding a family

For many of us, the period in our lives roughly between the ages of about 25 and 45 is the time when we find a partner and start a family. And I reckon the years spent raising children are some of the best times of your life. That's not to say it isn't challenging, though. Having kids can disrupt even the best-laid financial plans. Not only are there new mouths to feed, there is usually less money coming in, with one partner either leaving the workforce altogether or deciding to work casually or part-time. Despite this, I still think it really is a very special time in our lives and it just requires a bit of extra care to stay on course financially.

This chapter could probably form the basis of a book in itself, but I'll stick with what I believe are the key issues facing families these days – how to live with a mortgage (or, more accurately, how to best pay it off, since I firmly believe that owning your own home is one of the foundations of wealth); how to meet the costs of raising children, particularly funding their schooling; and, finally, putting aside some money for your retirement.

GIVE THE MORTGAGE ITS MARCHING ORDERS

In 1993 when the *Money* show first went to air, interest rates were around 9% and falling, and the key piece of advice being offered to homeowners was to maintain their mortgage repayments at the higher levels in order to pay off the home loan sooner. Ten years later, we have been lucky enough to have enjoyed several years of some of the lowest interest rates in decades. This may not have been cause for celebration among retirees or anyone else living off interest-bearing deposits, but it's been great news for homeowners. It pays to remember, though, that in the two decades or more that most of us take to pay off a mortgage, interest rates are likely to move through several cycles of ups and downs, and that a rise in interest rates, particularly once the international economy picks up, is inevitable sometime down the track. And with the banks reporting record levels of personal debt, even a small rise in interest rates could be a real squeeze. So, what do you do?

Well, the obvious answer is still to pay down the loan as quickly as possible. Look on it as beating the banks at their own game – paying extra amounts into the mortgage *before* interest rate rises occur. If you can manage the higher repayments, you'll pay your home loan off significantly sooner and save yourself a bundle in the process.

Size may matter in some areas of life, but when it comes to paying off your home loan, even small amounts can make a big difference. The key is to do it consistently, paying a bit extra on a regular basis. For example, pay an extra $10 each week off a $150 000 mortgage (at 7% over 25 years), and you can cut two years off the life of the mortgage and save almost $18 000 in interest.

Budget to find savings

Of course, it's easy to *talk* about making extra repayments. The question is, where will the money come from? Well, that's where budgeting comes in. When we first gave away a Budget Planner on the *Money* show, 60 000 people wrote in to get one. Why did so many people want one? Well, if you don't have a budget it's hard to save, and if you're not saving, the simple fact is that you're building someone else's wealth, and not your own. Now, you wouldn't be alone in doing this – a Commonwealth Bank report in 2002 estimated that around 37% of Australians are not saving. But doing a budget is vital to securing a comfortable future for your family, so I have included a Budget Planner at the end of the book. It's simple to use and the small amount of time taken to fill it out could be one of the best investments you'll ever make.

Your budget should pinpoint areas where you can make some savings. Now, I realise that for many families a bit of extra cash would be very welcome, but if you can cut back your expenditure and save a bit more, you can enjoy life without a mortgage far sooner.

Go for a shorter term

'For the term of his natural life' should be an expression reserved for convicts, not homeowners, and while you can spend a lot of time shopping around for the 'best' home loan, at the end of the day, the cheapest mortgage is often the one you pay off the fastest. Whether you opt for a longer or shorter term depends largely on the level of repayments you can afford, but bear in mind that what you 'save' in repayments today, you'll certainly make up for in interest later.

Let me explain. On a 25-year home loan of $200 000, for example, at an interest rate of 7% you can expect to pay more than $224 000 in interest over the life of the loan (this is on top of the principal of $200 000). But, if you took out the same mortgage, reducing the term to 15 years, your monthly repayments would rise by almost $400 a month, but you slash your total interest bill by over $100 000.

Twenty-five years is the standard mortgage term in Australia. And it's a time frame that's designed to correspond with our peak earning years. But if you want to get the mortgage monkey off your back sooner, think about a shorter term.

Make repayments fortnightly

If you're paying your mortgage off monthly but you feel like you're never getting ahead, you might want to consider paying fortnightly. Most mortgages require repayments to be made each month, meaning you make 12 repayments a year. However, if you make the simple change of paying *half* the normal monthly repayment every *fortnight*, you will end up making the equivalent of 13 monthly instalments every year – as there are 26 fortnights in a year. And this extra month's repayment each year can really make a difference to your mortgage without too much impact on the family budget.

Use an offset account

Saving extra cash in something like, say, a term deposit, just doesn't make financial sense if you have a mortgage. For every $1 you earn in interest on a deposit, you could lose almost half to the taxman, taking the gloss off already lacklustre returns on deposits. Using an 'interest offset account' can help overcome this.

When you use an offset account, the rate of interest you would normally earn on a deposit is set off against your mortgage. Here's how it works. Let's assume your home loan of $120 000 charges 7% interest, and you have an interest offset account (comprised of deposited cash) with a balance of $10 000. Instead of receiving interest on the deposit and paying interest on the full balance of the mortgage, the value of the offset account is deducted from (or 'offset' against) the amount outstanding on the mortgage. So, in this example, only $110 000 of the loan will be charged interest at 7%.

It's an arrangement that has significant tax advantages. As you have never actually received the interest on the cash in the offset account, it is not taxable. So you get the full benefit of the return without losing any to tax. And you pay off your mortgage faster.

The best offset accounts are those that offer the same rate of interest on both the deposit and the mortgage. This is known as a 'full offset', and it means that, in effect, you are getting a double-whammy return on your deposit as the rate is far higher than you would earn on a separate deposit account, plus you're getting it tax-free. On the downside, the banks compensate for this by charging a higher-than-average rate on the mortgage – usually around 0.10% to 0.15% more. So, if your mortgage is a big one and your savings are small, the higher variable rate that is charged on a full offset mortgage account can wipe out the benefits of this system altogether. You really need to do your sums to make sure it is worth your while.

Redraw facilities

A redraw facility lets you put any surplus cash into your mortgage instead of into a separate deposit. This reduces the amount of interest you pay – but gives you access to these extra repayments should you need them.

A number of redraw accounts let you treat your home loan as your main account. Your salary goes into it and you draw on it for living expenses. Every time that a large sum (like your weekly pay) is paid into the mortgage, it reduces the principal, which, in turn, reduces your interest bill.

The downside of redraw facilities is that you can only redraw if you are up-to-date with, or ahead of, your repayments. And in some cases you need to give the bank a few days notice to access the funds. However, if you are financially disciplined and can stick to a budget, it can be a great way to get more money into your home loan faster, and thereby pay it off earlier.

Work at it from Day One

The early years of your mortgage are when you can make the biggest difference over the term of the loan. For example, on a loan of $120 000 at 7% over 25 years, if you made a single extra repayment of $1000 in the first year, you would save around $4300 in interest and cut six months off the term of the loan. However, if you made the same payment in the fifth year of the loan, you would reduce the term by only four months and cut around $3000 from the interest bill – still welcome news, but not as effective as the earlier repayment.

Here's why. In the early years of a mortgage, the bulk of your repayments go towards meeting interest charges on the debt, as opposed to repaying the principal (the actual amount borrowed). It's only after the first five years that you'll begin to make some impact on the principal. But if you can make just a small extra payment at the beginning it comes straight off the principal, which then reduces the interest payable on the next payment.

Another tip (if the terms of the loan permit it) is to pay your first monthly repayment before it's due. Don't wait until a month after the date of settlement – get in early, and cut time and money from the loan.

Also, try to make your upfront fees just that – upfront. It can certainly be hard to get the extra cash to cover initial mortgage fees, so many borrowers take up the option to add them to the loan. But just a small amount added to the initial principal can make a big difference, not to your monthly repayments, but to the total interest you pay over the term of the mortgage. As a rule of thumb, every $5000 that you have saved, rather than borrowed, will save you $1800 over ten years (assuming an interest rate of 6.5% per annum).

Do your homework, shop around and drive a bargain

For most of us, a mortgage isn't just the biggest debt we'll ever have, it's also the longest. So it really pays to take the time to shop around to find the one that suits you best. When it comes to a mortgage, a hasty decision could cost you thousands of dollars.

Since banking deregulation in the 1980s, a lot of new players have entered the mortgage game and they are all keen to get your business. Some will negotiate on advertised rates and features, so it's well worth your while to ask a potential lender for their best deal, or whether they'll match, or better, another lender's offer.

The increasing number of lenders have bought with them a plethora of different mortgage structures. Where once there was a standard housing loan, these days you can choose from fixed-rate loans, capped loans and interest-only loans, to name a few. The key to finding the loan that suits you best is to look past the glossy advertising and get back to basics.

If you're looking for a standard variable rate home loan, web sites like www.bankchoice.com.au list the interest rates and charges for a huge selection of lenders. It also offers online calculators you can use to get an idea of what the repayments will be at different interest rates and terms. In addition, research group Cannex conducts regular reviews of over 2000 mortgages, giving each one a rating which is then reported on their web site at www.cannex.com.au. You can also find home loan rates in the financial press and in magazines like *Money*.

If you're after a mortgage with a few more bells and whistles, you may want to consider using a mortgage broker. These days about a third of us choose a home loan this way, but make sure the loan the broker suggests is the one that best suits you – not your broker. Mortgage brokers are sometimes paid a commission by lenders, so the loan recommended to you may be the one that pays the highest commission instead of being the one most appropriate to your needs.

With over 4000 mortgage brokers in the market, there's certainly plenty to choose from. My advice here is to go for a broker who isn't tied to any particular lender. And don't hesitate to ask what sort of commissions he or she is getting.

WHEN INTEREST RATES RISE

Don't fall for a quick fix

The words 'interest rate rise' have the same effect on homeowners as the expression 'iceberg ahead' has on cruise-ship passengers. While the urge to panic is understandable, there may be little to be gained by locking in to a fixed interest rate. And while you can agonise forever about whether or not to lock in a fixed rate, you'll find that interest rate predictions are notoriously inaccurate. Even the best-informed people get it wrong. A friend of mine, a financial director of a major Australian company, took out a fixed-rate mortgage in 1990, locking in at 15% for three years. He then sat by, scratching his head, while standard variable (bank) home loan rates dropped 15 consecutive times to a low of 8.75% in September 1993. His decision to take a fixed-rate loan could not have been more ill-timed – and he is a financial professional! In addition, locking into a fixed rate usually means you can't make those vital extra repayments.

Rather than fix the whole loan, it may be better to have a split loan, which combines a fixed-rate portion and a variable rate portion. This gives you the ability to make extra repayments with the security of a fixed component should rates rise.

Refinancing

The money-lending business these days is a bit like a smorgasbord where the consumer has a big choice of loans. So, if you think you can get a better deal on your home loan, think about switching to another lender.

Refinancing a mortgage will normally cost you around $1000 but it can go higher. Expect to pay a few hundred dollars in valuation fees, as well as an early discharge fee payable to your old lender. You could also be charged stamp duty on the new mortgage, depending on where you live, and if you borrow more than 80% of the property's value, you'll be up for mortgage insurance, payable at around 1% of the value of your property.

That said, if you see a better offer and you think there's money to be saved, do your numbers, or get your lender to do them for you.

Look for the 'true interest rate'

Many lenders charge administration fees on home loans. Not only do these bump up the cost of the loan, they also make it hard to compare between lenders. So, don't just look at the advertised interest rate. Ask your lender what the 'average annual percentage rate' (AAPR) or 'true rate' is on the loan. This figure takes into account all the costs of the loan, including upfront and ongoing fees, making it a far better guide to use when you're comparing mortgages.

More ways to save on your mortgage

- Save a bigger deposit. This includes saving for stamp duty, legal fees and the cost of building inspections.
- Don't pay for loan features you are unlikely to use.
- Make sure there are no penalties for extra repayments or an early payout.
- Look for 'portability' – being able to switch the loan from one property to another without incurring fees.
- See if your profession gets you a discount – some banks offer discounts and special packages to members of professional organisations.

MEETING THE COSTS OF PARENTHOOD

Children may be small fry, but they certainly aren't small change. And while we all want the best for our children, raising a family is an expensive business. In fact, according to a study* by the National Centre of Social and Economic Modelling (NATSEM), the cost of raising a child ranges from 9% to 31% of a family's income, and by the time your child turns 15, in addition to count-less grey hairs, they will have cost you around $140 000.

And children tend to get more expensive as they get older. The same study showed that a family on a gross weekly income of $810 will spend around $86 per week on their child while they are a pre-schooler, about $99 a week while the child is at primary school, and by the time that same child is in their teenage years, they'll be costing you around $178 a week. And, as experi-enced parents know, the more we earn, the more we spend on our kids, with only minor savings to be had with each subsequent child.

The arrival of children is always good news, but it often spells the end, even if it's just temporary, to being a two-income house-hold. Together with the extra cost, this can leave the household budget pretty stretched, adding additional stress on the family at a time when you just don't need it. Fortunately, though, children don't arrive overnight and we usually have a least a few months notice that the family is about to expand, which gives you valu-able time to prepare.

If you are part of a couple, saving as much as you can from one income and living off the other well before the birth of your baby not only gives you the chance to build a cash reserve, it can also be a wake-up call for what lies ahead. It's not a great idea to enter parenthood lumbered with a load of high-interest debt, so try to pay

* R. Percival & A. Harding, 'The Public and Private Costs of Children in Australia', National Centre of Social and Economic Modelling, University of Canberra, 2000.

off any personal loans or credit cards before the big event.

When parents-to-be are shopping for their baby, it is important to bear in mind that any purchases made on credit may be repaid out of a reduced income following the arrival of the baby. So, be especially wary of those offers that let you 'buy now and pay later'. They're not a problem if you can pay the full balance at the end of the interest-free period. But to be able to do this you need to have the discipline to save the full amount owing, which can be a real struggle when the household income is reduced – even if it is only for a short period during maternity leave. If you can't pay off the balance, you may find yourself facing interest rates approaching 30% (more on this in Chapter 4).

On the plus side, having one parent on a reduced income also gives you the opportunity to split part of your income and quite legitimately save a few dollars in tax. Let's say, for example, that a couple have $5000 in a term deposit returning 5%, which earns $250 per annum in interest. If the deposit is in the name of partner A, who is on an annual income of $38 000, the taxman will take a cut of 31.5%, or $79 of the interest, leaving only $171 as the after-tax return. This reduces the return the couple are getting on their money to around 3%. On the other hand, if the money is held in the name of partner B, who is a homemaker earning no other income, the couple can take advantage of the tax-free threshold and pay no tax on their interest.

If you want to deliver the baby in a private hospital, make sure you have private health cover in place well before the pregnancy occurs, as health funds often have a waiting period before you can make a claim.

Maternity leave from the mortgage

Your income may reduce when children come along, but the bills certainly don't. So it can be a challenge to keep kicking goals with the mortgage while living on less. But there are solutions. Some of our larger banks offer 'maternity leave' on mortgages, meaning you can reduce your repayments for an agreed period. Now, while this may relieve some of the financial pressure, it should only be seen as a short-term measure and I can really only recommend it for families where maternity leave of less than a year is being taken. You see, reducing the payments comes at the cost of extending your mortgage. In addition, the option isn't usually offered if you've only recently taken out your home loan.

Other alternatives to relieve the pressure include a period of interest-only payments or redrawing on excess payments you have made prior to taking maternity leave. Again, these should be regarded as only temporary solutions as none of them will make in-roads into paying out the mortgage altogether – which is the best form of relief there is!

GOVERNMENT ENTITLEMENTS FOR FAMILIES

Whenever you reach a crossroads in your life it's a good idea to take stock, and having children certainly fits the bill as one of the biggest crossroads you are likely to encounter. And while starting a family can be a real strain, many Australian families could be thousands of dollars better off if they accessed the family support payments available from the government. The chances are that there are benefits in the system that you could be due; however, for many people, wading through and trying to make sense of the paperwork is a daunting task – one that often falls into the too-hard basket.

It can be well worth the effort, though, as for families with children, there is a pool of money to tap into. To see how the government can help, let's look at the main types of support available for families.

Family Tax Benefit – Part A

This is mainly designed for families with children up to age 20 and your entitlement depends on your income. The current (March 2003) rates for Family Tax Benefit A are set out at the end of the chapter, but to receive the maximum amount of $3303 per year for a child under 13, your family income must be below $30 806. If you earn more than this, your payment reduces by 30 cents for each dollar over $30 806 until you reach the base rate of the Part A Benefit. You can earn up to about $83 000 (or more depending on how many children you have) before the Family Tax Benefit cuts out altogether. It is not the easiest entitlement to work out, though, so your best bet is to contact Centrelink to see what, if any, payment you are due.

Family Tax Benefit – Part B

This benefit is designed to help families on a single income, including sole parents. So, if your partner has lost their job, or you've separated, it's worth checking to make sure you're not missing out on the money. The maximum payment is $2836 each year for a child under five. Single parents get the full benefit regardless of their income, but in two-parent families, the parent on a lower income can earn up to $1752 annually before the benefit is reduced.

Both types of Family Benefit payments can be taken as fortnightly payments, as a lump sum, or you can opt to take it as a reduction in the tax withheld from your weekly wage or salary.

Parenting Payment

The Parenting Payment provides support for low-income families. Single parents, for example, can receive around $440 per fortnight (March 2003 rate), but the payment is subject to both an income and an assets test.

If you are struggling through single parenthood, have a look at Chapter 8, and do get in touch with Centrelink, because other benefits such as rent assistance may also be available to you.

Maternity Allowance

If you qualify for the Family Tax Benefit, the government will also give you a one-off lump sum Maternity Allowance of about $800 on the birth of your child. Note it is also paid for second and subsequent children, and may also be available for adopted children. The payment isn't assets tested, but you must apply for it within 26 weeks of your child's birth or you'll miss out.

Maternity Immunisation Allowance

This is a one-off lump sum payment of $208 for children aged 18 to 24 months who've had all their shots.

First Child Tax Refund or 'baby bonus'

The First Child Tax Refund or, as most people prefer to call it, the 'baby bonus', gives new mums a tax break of up to $2500 a year for a maximum of five years.

For example, if you earn a salary of $30 000 in the year before you stop work to have the baby, you would be taxed to the tune of $5380. With the baby bonus, you can treat that income as if it were spread over five years, and following the birth of your baby, claim back the tax you have paid in five annual instalments of $1076 each.

The bonus is capped at $2500 annually. This means that if you earn over $45 400, you won't get every penny of your tax back, but, at the other end of the scale, even if your income is less than $25 000, you'll still be entitled to the minimum annual bonus of $500.

If you return to work on a part-time basis you'll still be eligible for the bonus, but it will be reduced according to your income. All families have different needs, but don't let the reduction in the bonus turn you off going back to work. Extended periods away from the workforce can make it harder to get back into a job further down the track. A better option may be to think about part-time work, which will have less impact on the baby bonus, while keeping your job skills up to date.

If you haven't factored the bonus into the family budget, it's not a bad idea to use it to top up your super. The government will let you contribute the bonus without you having to meet any employment criteria. For more on spouse super, see page 63.

Child Care Benefit

This benefit can give eligible parents a rebate of around $2.60 an hour for money they've outlaid on child care. That makes it worth up to $133 a week for one child, but there are plenty of strings attached. You're only eligible for the maximum if your combined income is less than $30 000 annually, and if your child uses an 'approved' (professional) child care service. A lower amount is paid if your children are at school. This benefit is paid through the Family Assistance Office (FAO) and the number to call for more information is 136 150.

FUNDING YOUR CHILD'S EDUCATION

Like most parents, the cost of raising my young children was not uppermost in my mind when they arrived on the scene. But, as any parent with school-aged children will know, when they start out on the long road of schooling, those initial outlays for a pram and nappies are a drop in the ocean compared to what lies ahead. So, the tears you wipe away on your child's first day at school may well be your own when you see how much it's all going to cost.

Whether it's at a public or private school, the cost of education is rising. And while it can be as low as a few hundred dollars per year at the local public school, you can expect to pay in excess of $12 000 annually at some of our top private schools. Add on extras like coaching, sports activities and even laptop computers, and you begin to see how a relatively small person can generate a very large bill.

Setting aside money for your child's education was unheard of a few decades ago, but these days around 30% of Australian school students attend fee-based private schools. And the Australian Bureau of Statistics (ABS) reckons more than one-third of these students come from families earning under $42 000 per annum – with one parent often working just to pay for the kids' schooling.

But you don't have to second-mortgage the family home to give your kids a first-rate education. Selective government high schools hold annual entry exams and, for the successful few, these schools with their consistently good academic records offer an outstanding education for the bargain price of a few hundred dollars in 'voluntary contributions'. Most of the private schools also offer scholarships in varying forms, although these are hotly contested.

Given the degree of competition involved, it could be unrealistic to assume your child will be awarded a fee-exempt scholarship. So, instead of hoping that a lottery ticket comes good, the trick to paying for your child's schooling is to start putting money aside early, and letting compounding returns (earning interest on your interest) do the hard work for you.

Many parents put their child's name down at a private school shortly after birth, and it's not a bad idea to start investing for their education at the same time. But it pays to remember that funding an education is a long-term process. It takes time for the power of compounding to really kick in, and depending on the age of your child, you should be aiming for good capital growth rather than a steady income stream.

The first thing you need to do is review the family budget to work out what you can comfortably contribute on a regular basis (you'll find a Budget Planner to help with this at the end of this book). Alternatively, you can estimate the total cost of schooling and work backwards from this to determine what you need to put away on a monthly basis (just be sure to have a stiff drink on hand when you see the outcome).

Let's say, for example, that you plan to put your child through six years of private secondary schooling (commencing at age 12), at an annual cost of $8000. Assuming a return on your investments of 5% per annum (for the sake of simplicity I'll ignore inflation – but note that historically many private school fee increases outpace the rate of inflation), you'll need to put aside a minimum of about $170 each month from the day your child is born right through to when they finish high school to meet the cost. However, if you leave starting the savings regime until they enter primary school at age five, the monthly saving swells to around $250. Wait until your child is 11 and the investment climbs to about $670 each month. With the majority of families in Australia living on a combined gross income somewhere between $25 000 and $50 000, you begin to see why it pays to start saving early to pay for private school fees.

Having worked out how much you can set aside, you need to determine an investment strategy. Make sure it's one you can comfortably live with, as a change of plan mid-stream can cost you dearly in terms of capital gains tax and transaction costs. Remember, it's not enough just to put money away for the kids' education. You've got to put it to work, and if you've got a reasonable time frame (say, around seven to ten years), that means opting for growth assets like shares, property or a managed fund investing in these.

YOUR INVESTMENT STRATEGY

Strategy 1 – Do-it-yourself investing

Many people feel comfortable with the do-it-yourself (DIY) option. You have control over where you invest, flexibility in your choice of investments, access to the money if you need it in an emergency, and provided you hold the investment for over 12 months, you'll get a 50% discount on any capital gains you make. The downside is that you need to be sufficiently self-disciplined so that you don't dip into the money or panic-sell following short-term market downturns.

If you give yourself plenty of time by investing when the kids are young, you can afford to go for growth assets like shares, both domestic and international, and property. These investments carry more risk and are prone to short-term fluctuations, but over time you're likely to earn a better return than if you put the money into a term deposit.

When it comes to education costs, you will be paying lump sums like school fees on an annual basis. So, ideally you should look for an investment that lets you gradually draw down these amounts leaving the bulk of the funds working for you. Shares and managed funds fit this bill, but the same can't really be said of direct property – it's not as though you can sell off one of the bedrooms to pay for a year's worth of school fees. Having said that, you can certainly get access to the property market through listed property trusts and other managed investments where the underlying assets include property.

The investments I look at here fit the DIY bill, but the list certainly isn't exhaustive. What I need to stress is the importance of choosing quality, mainstream assets. Steer clear of anything promising over-the-top returns or being offered by an organisation you're not familiar or comfortable with.

Managed funds The downside to DIY investing is that unless you have a sizeable amount to invest, it's unlikely you'll get a good spread of investments, which leaves you more exposed to market jitters. There's also the dilemma of which shares or property to buy. If you are the sort of parent who would rather spend time playing with the kids than playing the stock market, managed funds may be a better alternative. Also known as unit trusts, managed funds pool investors' contributions into a range of investments, which are then managed as one big portfolio. If you've got a reasonable time frame, the principle of investing in growth assets still applies to managed investments, so go for a 'growth' fund. 'Balanced' funds often also have a high proportion of growth assets. If you don't have the luxury of time, consider more conservative 'capital stable' funds as they can sometimes outperform more volatile growth assets in the short term.

The downside to managed investments is that you can expect to pay ongoing management fees (called MERs) of about 2%. On the plus side, though, you can start with as little as $500 – especially if you opt for a regular investment plan (which I recommend), and you get far more diversification of underlying investments than if you go it alone.

Invest when your children are pre-schoolers and you give yourself a time frame of almost a decade to invest for secondary schooling, which means you can afford to go for a high-growth investment mix. As you get closer to the time when you need to draw on the funds, it's not a bad idea to transfer part of your investment into more conservative areas, such as a cash management account or term deposit. This strategy lets you redeem smaller amounts so your money keeps working for you for as long as possible, and your capital gains tax bill is spread out over time, keeping it manageable.

Endowment warrants If you feel comfortable investing in shares, but you don't have a large sum to invest, you may want to consider endowment warrants. These let you acquire shares at a future date, approximately ten years hence, by paying the issuer of the warrant a deposit based on today's share price.

You pay your initial deposit, anywhere between 30% and 65% of the share's current value, and what's left over is essentially a loan, secured against the shares. This outstanding amount, the difference between what you've paid and what the share was trading at on the day you invested in the endowment warrant, is increased by interest charged against it and reduced by dividends paid into it. The idea is that over time, the dividends will gradually eliminate the debt – the value of the dividends hopefully being greater than the interest charged, and that finally you will own the shares outright. So, if all goes well, your initial deposit may be the only payment you ever make.

Now, if after ten years the outstanding amount has not been reduced to zero, you can either pay one final instalment to own the shares entirely, or cash out the warrant with the issuer and receive the value of the shares at the current market price, less the outstanding amount (plus costs).

Another option with endowment warrants, if you need the money, is to trade them at any stage on the share market, their value being approximately equivalent to the current share price, less the amount outstanding.

Overall, there are a number of factors which impact on the performance of endowment warrants, with dividends and interest rates being the main ones. If the dividends are lower than expected, the value of the warrants will decrease, as lower dividends won't fully fund the amount outstanding. Of course, the opposite is also true – stronger than expected dividends will pay the amount outstanding earlier.

Also, if interest rates rise, it will take longer to pay the balance off. As the outstanding amount is essentially a loan, if interest rates rise, endowment warrant values will fall, and vice versa.

Finally, the value of endowment warrants moves up and down in concert with share price movements. So, if a share does well (or badly), the endowment warrant will too.

There are a number of positives associated with warrants. Primarily, you get to capture all the benefits of a share's dividends plus all of its capital growth without having to pay the full price for that share. And no capital gains tax is payable until you sell the shares or your endowment warrants. Finally, once you've invested, there's no paperwork to worry about, and with no administrative headaches, you can just put them in a drawer and forget about them for ten years.

The main downside to warrants is the possibility of losing the entire investment through a major share reversal. With any 'leveraged' investment (meaning one which is partly funded by borrowings as endowment warrants are), the beneficial effects of upward market movements are magnified, as are the negative effects of any downward movements. Secondly, there are no tax deductions on the interest paid as there would be if you took out a normal loan to buy some shares.

If you are thinking about using endowment warrants to save for your child's education, it may be a good idea to get some professional advice in selecting the shares, unless you have a pretty good grasp of the share market.

Insurance bonds Once a popular long-term investment, insurance bonds fell out of favour with many investors when the government earmarked them for tax changes in 1999. They were due to be taxed in much the same way as companies, but these plans were shelved in May 2002. This uncertainty about taxation has led to a drop in the number of providers offering insurance bonds, but as they can provide tax advantages to high-income earners, they could make a comeback.

When you invest in an insurance bond, the life insurance company or friendly society pays tax on the investment income at the rate of 30% each year. Provided you hold the bond for at least ten years, the proceeds are paid to you with no further tax payable. So, while insurance bonds are certainly not tax-free, they are tax-paid.

All the earnings of insurance bonds are reinvested, so they are very much a 'set and forget' type of investment. There is no distribution or dividend made during the life of the bond, meaning your funds are well and truly stashed away. If you do need to get your money out before the full ten years is up, you'll pay tax on part of the income (depending on how long you've held the bond for), getting a rebate for the 30% tax already paid by the life insurance company or friendly society that issued the bond.

No investment decision should ever be based on a tax benefit alone. Even high-income earners should look at the underlying investment portfolio of the bonds to make sure that the assets look reasonable (in other words, ones that look like they should be able to generate a reasonable return, including some capital growth).

Strategy 2 – Scholarship funds/education bonds

If you don't trust yourself to use the funds for education, there are alternatives. One option is to use an investment specifically earmarked for meeting education costs. These include things like education bonds, scholarship plans and other products marketed as investments designed to pay for education, both secondary and tertiary.

Scholarship plans are a form of forced saving once you have signed up, with many families contributing around $20 each week, often from the time their child is born. Some of these scholarship plans also offer career advice, academic motivation and even assistance to families in financial difficulty.

However, I see a couple of drawbacks with these plans. First of all, the funds can only be used for education and are not readily accessible in the short term – or in the event of an emergency. The same can be said of an investment property, but at least here you have a choice in the underlying assets, which is not the case with scholarship plans. Secondly, in the past these plans have invested in conservative (low risk, low return) assets rather than growth assets. This is certainly changing, but be aware that you may be able to get a better return and more flexibility by investing elsewhere.

Strategy 3 – Children's saving accounts

If you're serious about accumulating substantial funds, children's saving accounts are *not* a good option. They may be useful for teaching children about the value of money and how to save responsibly, and they are often fee-free, but the low rates of interest (often just a whisker above zero) that accrue on these accounts mean your child's nest egg may not even keep pace with inflation.

WHOSE NAME TO INVEST IN?

Having worked out how much to put away and where to invest your money, the question remains as to whose name the investment should be held in. Make a mistake here and it can cost you dearly in ongoing income tax, capital gains tax and even stamp duty if you change the investment over to another name.

Don't be tempted to invest in the name of your child, as unearned (investment) income of minors is taxed at 66% once it exceeds $416 a year. (However, this amount can rise to $643 if you include low-income tax offsets.)

There is no clear 'best' option here as the most appropriate course depends on the income of both parents and their children. The wisest approach is often for parents to hold the investments in their own name, in trust for the child. A parent who is out of the workforce or on a lower income is a more tax-effective trustee as they are more likely to have a lower marginal tax rate.

Family trusts may be viable for protection of family assets but their days as an income-splitting vehicle (to minimise tax) may be numbered. Proposed legislation that would have seen family discretionary trusts taxed as companies from July 2001 has been dropped, but there's no doubt that changes to the way trusts are taxed are still very much on the government's agenda. In addition, setting up a trust with a corporate trustee will cost around $1800, none of which is tax deductible, so you need sizeable investments to make the cost worthwhile. Putting investments in the name of the parent with the lower income is often a cheaper option than setting up a family trust.

With the best of intentions in mind, grandparents often want to gift amounts to grandchildren, or at least hold investments in their name. Unfortunately, both these strategies are fraught with difficulty as they may affect any pension entitlements.

WHAT IF I'VE LEFT IT TOO LATE?

If your children have already reached school age and you haven't started investing for their education, you need to consider some alternative strategies. Your investment time frame is shorter, so conservative, interest-based investments are more appropriate. They won't give you stellar returns, but you won't have to wait for the value of your investment to recover from the inevitable market dips that affect growth assets in the short term.

For some parents, it may be more a question of meeting school payments rather than saving for them. Here, too, there are a number of alternatives. One is to borrow the money, possibly through a personal loan, or more preferably, using a mortgage redraw facility, with its lower interest rates. This allows you to take advantage of discounts on upfront payment of school fees, but you'll need to weigh this up against the possibly long-term expense of interest on the extra amount borrowed.

PLAN FOR THE FUTURE – SUPERANNUATION

I mentioned at the start of this chapter that these are also the years of your life when you should start to give serious thought to laying the foundations for a comfortable retirement. Paying off your mortgage should be a priority, and if you can get rid of at least a significant chunk of your home loan by the time you are 50, you'll certainly be in a good position to kick some real financial goals.

But while your house is important, it shouldn't be your only financial asset. A lot of people think they can get through to retirement, sell the house and buy something smaller. But with retirees living longer and having higher expectations of retirement, this may not be enough. So, what else should you be doing when you are thirty-something and married with children? The answer is *putting money away in super*. I reckon your home and your super are your two most important financial concerns, but it's a question of balance. You have to enjoy life with your children and that will cost money, but you can't sacrifice your future.

There probably aren't many subjects more impenetrable, eye-glazing or confounding than superannuation, but it still needs to be mentioned in this chapter, because if you can start putting some money into super now, you have a much longer period to let compounding returns work their magic. And if you want a comfortable retirement, as a couple you will need a combined annual income of at least $25 000 a year. This will allow you to maintain your own home, afford a small car, take local holidays and eat out now and then. But you need to work at building the nest egg that will pay you even this basic level of retirement income.

As a rule of thumb, you can work out how much capital you will need in retirement by multiplying your required income by 17 for an age 55 retirement; 15 for an age 60 retirement; and 13 for an age 65 retirement. So, for example, if you require an annual retirement income of $25 000, you'll need:

Retire at	Nest egg needed
Age 55	$425 000
Age 60	$375 000
Age 65	$325 000

If you're an employee and earning more than $450 per month, your employer, under the Superannuation Guarantee, should be making compulsory contributions into a super fund for you at 9% of your gross income. While employers aren't exactly crazy about this, these contributions are great for employees. After all, who wouldn't be happy having someone else put money away into a reasonable investment for you? However, according to the Association of Super Funds of Australia (ASFA), someone earning around the average weekly wage before retirement and contributing 9% of their wages to super for 30 years would end up with a total retirement income of only $19 000 a year – and that includes a part-pension. This is way short of the income most of us would like to retire on.

I suggest that contributions of 15% of your salary over your working life is what most Australians need to retire on comfortably. Now this may sound like a lot, and it may be more than you can afford to commit to super at the moment, but even a few dollars invested *now* can make a big difference, and for my money, one of the best ways to get ahead is to 'salary sacrifice'. This simply means that you contribute money into super from your wage *before* you pay tax. This way, instead of the taxman taking about 48.5 cents out of every dollar if you are in the highest tax bracket, he only takes 15 cents (super contributions being taxed at 15%). So for every $1000 you direct into superannuation via salary sacrifice, $850 actually gets invested as opposed to $515 if you didn't salary sacrifice and took it as cash and then invested that.

The table opposite shows just how tax-effective salary sacrifice can be. In this example, paying $2000 into your super through salary sacrifice will see you $630 *better off* each year than if you pay the same amount out of your take-home pay.

	Super paid by salary sacrifice	Super paid out of after-tax salary
Gross income	$35 000	$35 000
Less super contribution	$2 000	N/A
Taxable income	$33 000	$35 000
Less income tax and Medicare of 1.5%	$6 775	$7 405
After-tax income	$26 225	$27 595
Less super contribution	N/A	$2 000
Disposable income	$26 225	$25 595
Gain from salary sacrifice	$630	N/A

How tax-effective salary sacrifice is will depend on your tax rate. For the 2002/03 year this is how it works:

Taxable income	Tax rate
$0–$6000	0%
$6000–$20 000	17%
$20 001–$50 000	30%
$50 001–$60 000	42%
$60 001+	47%

Note, though, that if you earn over $90 527 per annum and you salary sacrifice, you pay the 15% contributions' tax plus an additional sliding surcharge. This surcharge stops at a maximum 15% additional when your earnings are over $109 924. The government is talking about reducing the top rate of the surcharge until it reaches 10.5% in 2004/05, but in early 2003 this plan is still in the pipeline.

Spouse super

When a parent is at home looking after children, they are not getting the benefit of employer-sponsored super, and this is a real concern, especially for women. On average, women have far less in super than men (owing mainly to the years spent raising children), and projections show that even in thirty years' time the average super balance for women will still only be around 70% of men's.

Apart from the inequality of the situation, making sure your spouse has a reasonable super nest egg can certainly give your retirement income a shot in the arm. Firstly, it overcomes the problem where one partner has little or no super while the other is approaching what's known as the 'reasonable benefits limit', which is the maximum you can have in super before you cop some pretty hefty tax rates. Secondly, it gives you more opportunities to split your retirement income, which helps to reduce your tax bill. There are two simple ways to improve your spouse's super: using the spouse super rebate or splitting your super contributions.

Spouse super rebate

The spouse superannuation rebate lets you claim an 18% tax rebate if you contribute to a spouse's super fund. You can get the rebate for contributions up to $3000 each year, but the rebate can only be claimed if your spouse is a homemaker earning less than $13 800 annually. You can contribute more, but you won't get a rebate for contributions over $3000.

Splitting super contributions

From July 2003, couples may be able to have their personal and 50% of their employer super contributions paid into a separate account in the name of their non-working or low-income spouse. The benefit of this is that a couple can get two reasonable bene-fits limits and tax-free thresholds when they retire. Note, though, that for people with small super balances, or who are contribut-ing small amounts, the second set of fees and charges you will pay in an extra super fund could erode your retirement savings. So it is worth getting some professional advice to see if this option is right for your circumstances.

Super for children

These days you can make super contributions (up to $3000 over three-year periods) for your child. The only upside to this idea is that by the time your child has retired some sixty or so years hence, your super contributions may have grown to a darn good nest egg. But let's be realistic here. In the last 15 years, super-annuation has undergone enormous tax and legislative changes, so goodness only knows what's coming up over the next half-century. As if that's not bad enough, there are no tax breaks for the child or the person making the contributions. So it's hard to see people leaping into this and I reckon most of us would be far more interested in investing for our child's education (either secondary or tertiary) than investing for their old age (their children's that is, not their own).

INVESTMENT TIPS FOR FAMILIES

Do

- make additional repayments on your mortgage
- aim to put 5% or even 10% of your income into both your and your partner's super, preferably by salary sacrifice
- have a clear plan to achieve your financial goals
- start to make plans for the next stage of your life
- protect your assets, your income and your life with insurance – but don't double up. Many super policies already include life insurance and other benefits
- be realistic about the amount of money you will need to be independent once you stop work
- pay off non tax-deductible debts (home loans, credit cards, personal loans) before tax-deductible investment loans (see Chapter 4 for more on this)
- make a will and update it every five years or following a change in your family situation
- enjoy the family years – they are over all too quickly.

Don't

- panic – it's never too late to start making plans and investing for them
- start spending all the mortgage repayments on lifestyle pursuits once the house is paid off
- use any increase in your wage or salary just to fund a more expensive lifestyle.

Maximum rate of Family Tax Benefit – Part A

For each child	Fortnightly amount	Annual amount
Less than 13 years	$126	$3303
13 to 15 years	$160	$4190
16 to 17 years	$40	$1062
18 to 24 years	$54	$1427

Source: Centrelink, as at March 2003.

Base rate of Family Tax Benefit – Part A

For each child	Fortnightly amount	Annual amount
Less than 18 years	$40	$1062
18 to 24 years	$54	$1427

Source: Centrelink, as at March 2003.

Maximum rate of Family Tax Benefit – Part B

For each child	Fortnightly amount	Annual amount
Less than 5 years	$108	$2836
5 to 15 years (or 16 to 18 if a full-time student)	$75	$1978

Source: Centrelink, as at March 2003.

Digging your way out of debt

No one likes being in debt, but going into the red is, for many of us, necessary to reach our financial goals. After all, if we weren't able to borrow money, most of us would not be able to buy a home to live in – which I strongly believe is one of the cornerstones of wealth. However, what is worrying is that our total household debt has doubled in the last decade. On average, every Australian is now indebted to the tune of $39 000, a figure that includes all personal loans, credit cards and mortgages. This is nothing to be sneezed at – especially when you consider that this figure is spread across every man, woman and child in the country.

But, the interesting thing is, not *all* debt is bad. I'll run through the four main types of debt, and you'll see how, in some cases, it can actually make financial sense to be in debt. I call these four types of debt:

- 'effective' debt
- 'happily necessary' debt

- 'sadly necessary' debt, and
- 'disastrous' debt.

'Effective' or good debt has two important characteristics. First, it is used to buy assets whose value will grow over the long term (like property, shares or a business); and second, because the assets are used to generate income, the interest payments on it are tax deductible – thereby reducing the real cost of the loan.

Here's how it works. Let's say you borrow money to buy an investment property. You pay 6.5% interest on the loan, but the property earns an annual return of 4%, which brings your out of pocket payments back to 2.5%. However, this cost is further reduced because you're able to claim a tax deduction for the interest. In this example, if you are earning up to $50 000, the real cost of the loan falls to 1.7%. If you're earning up to $60 000, the real cost of the loan is about 1.4%, and if you earn more than $60 000, the real cost drops to 1.2%. And this remaining cost should be more than covered by the increase in the value of the investment property over the long run.

But the key to making effective debt work for you is to do it sensibly and buy decent assets, and by that I mean ones with genuine prospects for growth, at the right price. If you can do this, there's really no reason why you should limit your effective debt. However, that's not to say that you should enter into it lightly. You need to think carefully about what would happen to you if interest rates rise; if the value of the asset falls; or if you lose your income through unemployment or illness. (Income protection insurance is a must if you have any sort of debt – more on this later.)

I encourage you to maintain effective debt for the longer term in areas where it is helping you to generate wealth, but even this type of debt should be paid off by the time you retire.

Next on the list is 'happily necessary' debt. This is usually at a relatively low interest rate and is used to buy an asset that is likely to increase in value, like your home. I'm comfortable with people taking out happily necessary debt because it's going towards what will be a worthwhile asset. At the end of the day, though, you still need to plan to get rid of this type of debt as soon as you can, as it can drain your financial resources.

'Sadly necessary' debts are those we rack up buying the things that most of us 'have to have', like, say, a car. Now, cars are terrible investments – they fall in value and cost heaps to run, but for most of us they are necessary for work and play. My best advice if you have this type of debt is to knuckle down and plan to get rid of it as soon as possible.

What I am really down on, though, is what I call 'disastrous debt'. Here, I'm talking about the high interest, easy to get hold of debt that encourages us to live beyond our means. It's the debt that's racked up using personal loans or credit cards to buy things like groceries, clothes, entertainment and holidays, all of which are here today and gone tomorrow. Using debt to buy items that have no real value is the equivalent of spending money you don't have. And it's this sort of debt that I'll be concentrating on in this chapter, simply because it's getting plenty of ordinary people into serious financial trouble.

GETTING YOUR MONEY UNDER CONTROL

Up until about the 1980s, if you wanted to buy something you had to save for it, or put it on lay-by. Back then, lenders were far more picky about who they lent money to. Then, in the 1980s, interest rates began to climb and lenders worked out that the number of people defaulting on things like credit cards would be more than compensated for by the income generated from interest and fees.

And they were absolutely right. Today, there are close to 17 million credit cards in circulation in Australia, each with an average balance of around $2330. Now I know there are many people out there who clear their credit cards each month, which means these figures don't tell the whole story. There must be heaps of people up to their eyeballs in debt. And, as anyone deep in debt can tell you, it is very hard to budget and save, let alone invest, when you've got different amounts of money being paid out all over the place. But perhaps the most serious issue facing people saddled with a lot of debt is that it leaves you vulnerable to falls in your income, either through illness or unemployment.

That's when the misery of having to go into hock to make ends meet arises. This can happen through paying for everything with your credit card, treating it as if it's cash (which it very much isn't), or by entering into personal loans you can't afford. But it doesn't have to be this way. There is a way out of bad debt.

Under normal circumstances, people get into debt for one main reason – they don't have control of their money. By this I mean, quite simply, that they spend more than they earn. It is easy to think that our debt problems could be overcome if our income was higher, but experience has taught me that nothing could be further from the truth. In general, the more we earn, the more we spend. People don't get into debt because they don't have enough money. They get into debt because they don't have enough *control* over their money – and this normally flows from spending more than they earn. Income rarely has anything to do with it – even if you are pulling in a million dollars a year, if you're spending a million and one, you're in trouble.

The trouble with debt

Debt is a double-edged sword. It lets us purchase things sooner rather than later, meaning we can take advantage of discounts and specials, but that convenience comes at a price. When you borrow to pay for things like a holiday (which is worth nothing in dollar terms the moment you get back), a stereo, clothes or furniture (which are practically worthless after three to five years) you pay interest on them, so they end up costing you more. No one would voluntarily pay an additional 16% on the things they purchase, yet this is just what you do if you stick with minimum repayments on the average credit card.

And every dollar you pay in interest is a dollar you could be saving and investing to build your own wealth – not your lender's.

The warning signs to watch for

We all like to think we can manage debt, but with increasing numbers of Australians turning to bankruptcy (24 000 in the 12 months to June 2002), it isn't always the case. In my experience, most people know when they are in debt over their heads – even if it's only a 'gut feeling'. Of course, there are some obvious signs that all is not well – like carting your valuables off to the local pawnbroker – but other signs are less clear. If you are unsure, take a look at the list below and even if only one of the warning signs sounds familiar, it could be time to take action.

- Regularly spending beyond your budget.
- Living from pay packet to pay packet.
- Having to borrow money from friends and family.
- Being unable to meet large, one-off expenses like car repairs.
- Making only the minimum repayments on your credit card each month.
- Using debt to repay debt – for example, using one credit card to repay another.
- Being at or near your credit card limit.
- Getting late payment notices for bills.
- Juggling funds between bank accounts in the hope that your spouse or partner doesn't discover the debt.
- Approaching non-mainstream, high-interest 'fringe' lenders for funds (see 'Pay day' lenders on page 81).

An alternative to this checklist is the approach used by the banks when they determine your eligibility for finance. Start by adding up all of your fixed monthly commitments including rent or mortgage repayments, plus credit card payments and any other loan repayments. If the combined total of these is more than around 30% of your gross (before tax) pay, it is time to cut back on your debt.

THE MAIN CAUSES OF DISASTROUS DEBT

Credit cards

When I grabbed a credit card from a person I was interviewing on the *Money* show in 1993 and chopped it into pieces, many viewers were shocked. But, a decade later, we are still finding that credit cards are ridiculously easy to obtain and to use, but horribly hard to pay off.

Credit cards charge some of the highest interest rates around, and my general advice on them is like the old saying about exercise: 'If you feel like becoming involved, lie down until the feeling goes away'. There is no doubt credit cards are very convenient, and can be a lot safer than carrying cash. And if you are travelling overseas they are particularly handy, especially in the USA, where credit cards are sometimes the only way you can pay. The problem, however, is that credit cards make spending easy. That makes saving hard, and unless you use them wisely you can quickly become lumbered with mounting debt. It's all about mastering your card – not allowing your card to master you!

How do credit cards work? Credit cards are basically a 'line of credit'. This means you borrow money from the card issuer when you make a purchase, and you can choose to either repay this amount in full each month or repay only part, but be charged interest on the amount outstanding. This balance is then carried over to the following month, together with any new purchases.

The number of credit cards on issue in Australia has increased eightfold since 1985 and with good reason. For the card providers, they are big money spinners. In addition to the hefty interest charges, the card issuer (Bankcard, Visa, MasterCard and American Express being the most widely used issuers) slugs the merchant for a percentage of the transaction. The average charge is about 2%, explaining why small retailers prefer to be paid in cash and often offer a discount for it (although these days new laws let retailers charge you for using a credit card). The card issuer also earns additional revenue by enclosing junk mail with your statement.

Card issuers use an extraordinarily complex system of accounting to come up with the interest charge. It is a system that I have long suspected is understood only by a small handful of eggheads, but, broadly speaking, interest is calculated either from the date of the monthly statement or from the date of purchase. Interest accrues immediately on cash advances, with some card issuers also charging a fee for this – in some cases around 1.5% on the full amount of the advance.

When you receive your statement you normally have 25 days (although it may be as few as 14) to pay your bill. You may have up to 55 days interest-free, during which no interest is charged – *if* you started from a $0 balance. The interest-free period generally goes out the window if you have an outstanding balance carried over from your last statement.

The interest charge becomes even harder to follow if you don't pay the statement out in full. Some cards charge interest on the outstanding amount calculated back to the items' purchase dates, not to the end of the interest-free period. And if you buy more on your credit card before you've paid the amount already owing, you may be charged interest from the date of the new purchases – in other words, no more interest-free period. Your interest-free period on any new purchases may not be reinstated until you have paid fully for all previous purchases.

If you have managed to stay with me to this point, well done – we've probably both earned (and need) a stiff drink – but there's more. The card issuer has no security over the outstanding balance (meaning they don't have a claim over one of your assets if you can't repay the debt), so the rate of interest is higher than for other forms of finance. And, unless you pay the full balance off each month, the effect of compounding interest (interest changed upon interest) can turn a minor debt into a mountainous one. (More on this later.)

Some card issuers also charge an annual 'membership' fee, which has always seemed a bit rich to me. The official line is that this fee is used to meet some of the issuer's expenses, but the fact is that it all goes to the card issuer's bottom line.

Affinity cards These are otherwise standard credit cards, the point of difference being that the card issuer usually links up with a particular charity or cause, making a donation every time you use the card to make a purchase. Now, I am certainly all for support-ing charities, but if you are tempted to apply for one of these cards just because of its connection to a good cause, you may be better off making a donation to your favourite charity and getting a tax deduction for it.

Store cards It is hard to find something good to say about these cards. Sure, the retailers who offer them promote benefits like reward programs, extended warranty periods and exclusive card-holder shopping evenings, but these marketing ploys are really designed to encourage you to spend more, and in many cases, to overspend. The sting in the tail is that these cards generally charge interest rates above even those of standard credit cards, and some cards will backdate interest charges to the date the goods were purchased if you fail to pay the balance off in full each month.

To make matters worse, these cards are easy to obtain, with application forms often placed near the cash register and approval for credit sometimes being given on the spot. And don't fall into the trap of thinking that a store card cements your relationship with your favourite shop. When you take out one of these cards, what you are doing is entering a finance agreement with a third party credit provider. For example, GE Capital Finance is the company behind the Coles Myer card. Something else to be wary of is the cardholder's 'exclusive shopping night'. Free champagne is often a feature at these events, and if you have a few drinks and then shop with your plastic, the resulting bills can be eye-watering. My advice regarding store cards is to really weigh up the benefits, if any, of being loyal to one particular retailer.

Charge cards Not all cards are created equal, and one to be wary of is the charge card. Principally offered by American Express and Diners Club, these cards *do not* offer an ongoing line of credit – when you receive your monthly bill you are expected to pay it out in full.

If you fail to pay the bill, the penalties are stiff. Some charge a late payment fee of $20 plus penalty interest on the outstanding balance of around 3% *each month*. That's the annual equivalent of over 40% interest after compounding. Fail to pay the monthly balance twice and your card may be cancelled. But the real trap with these cards is that there is often no pre-set credit limit, which can be a one-way ticket to financial disaster if you're tarred with the born-to-shop brush.

What the card issuers don't tell you The credit card issuer usually sets a minimum monthly repayment somewhere between 1.5% and 2.5% of the outstanding balance. Treating this as the minimum amount that you *should* pay, as opposed to the minimum that you *can* pay simply doesn't make good financial sense. You see, the issuer sets a minimum so that if you stick to it, it can take decades to pay off even relatively small sums.

Consider this. Bill decides to take a 'cheap' holiday to the Gold Coast. He pays for the air fare, hotel accommodation and a whole lot of crummy souvenirs to take home, using his credit card. All up, he puts $1000 on the plastic. The card carries an interest rate of 16% and has a minimum monthly repayment of 2% of the balance. Bill sticks to the minimum repayment as this makes the least immediate impact on his wallet. But by doing so, he will be paying off the trip for 187 months (that's over 15 years!), during which time he will have paid $1300 in interest – and that's assuming he never uses his card again! It would want to have been a darn good holiday.

It works this way because the minimum repayment on your card is set at a far lower percentage than the interest rate being charged. So, the magic of compounding interest is working, but it is working in favour of the card issuer – and against you. In Bill's case, the first year's repayments would total $231, but they barely make a dent on the outstanding balance, which after 12 months would still be $923. The only way around this is to pay more than the minimum required repayment or, better still, pay off the balance in full each month.

If you need a card

With hundreds of credit cards to choose from, it pays to shop around for the best deal. Low interest rates shouldn't be your only consideration, though. Sometimes card credits offer 'honeymoon rates' to attract new cardholders. These are rates that start out low but often catapult to a higher charge sometime down the track.

If you want to compare credit cards, research group Cannex conducts regular reviews of around 250 credit cards, giving each one a rating. These ratings can be seen on their web site at www.cannex.com.au.

Ten tips for using credit cards

1. Make sure you shop around and get a card appropriate to your needs. If you are *unlikely* to pay the balance out in full each month, go for a card with a low interest rate and a longer interest-free period. However, note that as a rule, the longer the interest-free period, the higher the interest rate. If you are *likely* to pay off the balance in full each month, the rate of interest isn't as important, so look for a card with low, or no, annual fees.
2. Read the fine print – additional fees add up.
3. Opt for a low credit limit and don't be tempted to increase it. Or, try setting your own spending limits on your card and stick to them.
4. Limit yourself to one card – it makes it easier to budget and harder to get into too much trouble. Using a second card to pay off the first only delays the inevitable financial meltdown.
5. Try not to carry any debt from one billing period to another – the cheapest interest rate is the one you don't pay at all! Pay off as much as you can manage. Certainly try to pay more than the minimum required repayment.
6. Consider a 'debit' card – they draw straight from your bank account. Better still, pay cash or use lay-by for those big-spending times of year like Christmas.
7. Be prepared to cut up your credit card if your spending gets out of control.
8. If self-control is not your strong suit, avoid charge cards – you could find them the most dangerous plastic of all.
9. Don't be tempted to get a credit card or use your existing card simply to get customer loyalty points. Research has continually shown that this can be a very expensive way to get 'free' rewards.

10. Never regard a credit card as cash in your pocket – it certainly isn't! Avoid cash advances – you will be hit with interest from the day you make the withdrawal, and not just on the cash advance but also on subsequent purchases, until you take the balance owing back to $0.

Personal loans

Of the thousands of letters I receive each year, around one-third are from people battling problems with personal loans. Whenever you contemplate taking out a personal loan, think very carefully about why you are doing it, because most purchases financed through personal loans leave you with no real asset, only a debt.

Broadly speaking, personal loans can be broken into two main types – 'secured' and 'unsecured'. A secured loan is one where the lender has security over one of your assets, such as a car or some other valuable item, until you have paid off the loan. An unsecured loan is one where the lender has no such security, and because of the relatively higher risk to the lender, unsecured loans are generally offered at higher interest rates.

If you default on a *secured* loan (meaning, you stop making repayments), the lender has the right to take possession of the secured asset and sell it to recoup the debt. Before they can do this, they need to send you a 'default notice' telling you why they are taking action, as well as advising you of any steps you can take to stop them. This notice gives you 30 days to either catch up with your payments or to renegotiate the debt with your creditor before they can take any further action. If the asset put up for security is kept on private property it can only be repossessed with the written permission of a person living there, or with a court order. In fact, if you have paid off at least 75% of the loan, your creditor will need the court's permission to repossess the asset.

If you default on an *unsecured* loan the lender generally has two options. If you owe more than $2000, they can apply to have you made bankrupt, although many lenders would rather renegotiate the loan repayments than take this step. If the amount owed is less than $2000, the lender can apply for a court order that allows the sheriff (this is the name for an officer of the court – don't expect to see Wyatt Earp gallop up) to take possession of sufficient assets to cover the debt. These are then sold at public auction with the proceeds going to the creditor.

Now, these provisions vary slightly between states, and your loan contract may set out specific provisions in the event that you fall behind with your repayments (so be sure to read it!) But come the crunch, whether your loan is secured or not, you can be forced to sell up to meet your debts. In either case, it is fairly drastic stuff and hopefully it's something you will never have to experience. Nevertheless, I'll be looking at what you should do in those circumstances a bit further on.

When you take out a personal loan Look, avoid taking out a personal loan to finance consumption if at all possible. But, if you must have one, it is worth trying to get the funds from a bank or credit union rather than a finance company, as bank/credit union rates are usually lower, sometimes dramatically so. And if you find yourself facing repayment difficulties, the large banks are less likely to push small debtors into bankruptcy because of concerns that this may tarnish their public image. Finance companies, on the other hand, are generally less concerned with public relations and can be more aggressive in chasing up outstanding debts.

Getting saddled with debt is easy. Paying it off is hard. So, before you sign up for a loan, make sure you can comfortably answer these questions:

- What is the interest rate?
- How long will it take to pay the loan off?
- What will the total cost of the loan be?

- Can I afford the weekly repayments?
- If I get a wage rise can I pay the loan off faster?
- Are there any penalties if I fall behind with my repayments?
- Will I be hit with penalties if I want to pay out the loan early?

Finally, ask yourself whether or not you really need the item. Take the cost of the interest into account when you make this decision, as it can take the shine off a 'bargain' very quickly. Let's say, for example, that Mike, aged 21, wants to buy a motorbike. The latest model is on 'sale', reduced from $11 000 to $10 000 – not a bad saving. Mike pays for it using a personal loan of $10 000 at 11% interest, to be paid off over three years. However, by the end of the loan he will have forked out $1785 in interest, which more than eats up the discount he got. On top of this, Mike will be paying monthly repayments of around $327 until the age of 24, making it hard for him to get started early with a savings plan.

Now, let's turn the tables around. We'll say Mike decides to catch the bus for a bit longer, and he *saves* that $327 each month for three years. Even if his money earned just 5% (which is possible with, say, an online savings account), he would end up with a nest egg of $12 672. Having the cash will give him far more bargaining power when he finally decides to buy a set of 'wheels', and it forms a good starting point to build *his* wealth – rather than his bank's.

'Interest-free' and 'no repayment' financing

This sort of 'buy now – pay later' financing has become all the rage among retailers in recent years. 'Buy now – pay an arm and a leg later' is more like it. You see, while these deals usually sound very generous, there's a catch. Unless you pay the full balance before the interest-free period expires, you can find yourself lumbered with a hefty loan at interest rates that make credit cards look cheap.

With interest-free financing, shoppers are invited to buy items like furniture or appliances on credit, where they are given a few months, or, in some cases, up to two years from the date of purchase, to pay for it using a regular repayments schedule. It all sounds very enticing, but there are a few stings in the tail with this sort of finance. Many hapless shoppers have discovered that the minimum repayments may not be enough to pay the loan out in full before the interest-free period comes to an end, and any outstanding balance at this point can be subject to interest rates high enough to give you vertigo. In most cases the interest will be levied on whatever is still owing, but in some cases, interest may be charged on the full price of the item, backdated to the date of purchase, regardless of how much of the debt has been paid off!

Let's say, for example, that you purchase outdoor furniture costing $2000 using one of these in-store 'interest-free' loans. There is no interest to pay for the first year, but after 12 months you have only managed to pay back $1300. At this point you could find yourself billed for one year's interest on the full $2000 purchase price, not on the $700 outstanding. With some of the rates on these offers being as high as 27%, you would now owe $1240 (being the outstanding $700 *plus* 12 months' interest of $540 on the original purchase price of $2000). And this amount is also attracting interest at 27%. This is a disastrous situation!

The secret with this seductive in-store financing is to be well aware that if you take it up, you could be pushing yourself deep into debt. You should really only consider these loans where you either have the funds on hand and can use this opportunity to earn interest on the cash before you have to pay the full balance, or if you are absolutely positive that you can save the full amount before the interest-free period expires.

'Pay day' lenders

With banks increasingly streamlining their services, many have found it uneconomic to make small, short-term loans, as the cost of the paperwork outweighs the relatively modest interest income. This has left a gap in the market for all manner of 'fringe' lenders and one of those is 'pay day' lenders.

These lenders let you borrow small sums to tide you over a short period – typically between one and four weeks – but what sets these lenders apart from others are the crippling finance charges. Costs of around $25 on a one-week loan of $100 are not uncommon. That equates to an annual interest rate of 1300%, making it 80 times more expensive than a cash advance on your credit card.

And if you fail to cough up the cash on the due day, you have the 'choice' of extending the loan and thereby racking up more fees, or using one of your other assets to pay off the debt. Some pay day lenders ask for a direct debit authority on your bank account before they hand over any cash, which lets them access your money before you do!

Recent reforms have meant that these lenders are now required to tell you upfront the annual rate of interest you are being charged. But the fact remains that the people who often turn to pay day lenders are those who can least afford their exorbitant rates. Before you even think about going to one of these lenders, I urge you to take a look below at my ten steps to getting out of debt. It has to be a lot cheaper than going for one of these extraordinarily expensive loans that often require nothing short of a miracle to stop you sliding deep into the red.

Never ignore notices or letters from creditors. If you come across anything you do not understand or that does not match your records, contact your creditor or a financial counselling service immediately.

TEN STEPS TO GETTING OUT OF DEBT

Most people don't suddenly find themselves deep in debt overnight. It generally takes time, building slowly at first. And just as it took time to get into debt, the best way to get back on top is also a gradual process. I'd like to say there was a quick way out, but just as building your wealth takes time, so does getting back on track.

1. Draw up a budget

Put simply, budgeting is the most effective tool there is to get and keep your finances under control. A budget tells you where your money is going, where you can cut back and where you can save. And once you have savings you can dig your way out of debt – and stay debt free.

To help you with this, I've included a Budget Planner at the back of this book. I recommend that you use it, as the prospects of you making an impact on your debt are remote unless you can cut back on your spending and start chiselling away at your debt.

I know this sounds easier said than done, especially for those of you on low incomes. And, yes, there's no denying that cutting back on your spending is difficult when there's very little fat to trim back in the first place. But no matter how much you earn, it is a question of taking control of your money. And this means managing your cash flow, which you can only do by budgeting.

A budget will also give you a much better idea of where your money is actually going. It is estimated that people regularly spend between $50 and $300 each month that they cannot account for. Yet this is money that could be used to help repay a debt.

The key to budgeting, though, is to keep it realistic. Most people significantly underestimate how much it costs them to live, and end up giving the budget the flick out of frustration after just a few weeks. It is better to err on the side of generosity when you draft a budget, and if you find you are making extra savings, regard them as a bonus (to save, not to spend!).

Once you have drafted your budget, it's a matter of reviewing it on a regular basis and finetuning it from there. Remember, the idea is to cut back on your spending so that you can channel the savings into reducing your debt. If that's not happening, it could be time to go back to the drawing board.

2. Work out your financial position

Sometimes, it's easy to feel overwhelmed by your debts, making it hard to see the 'big' picture. But when you take your overall financial health into account, things don't always look so grim. To get a clear picture of where you are now, make a list of your assets – everything you own – and compare their value to your liabilities – everything you owe. Use the market value of your assets (what they could be sold for), as you may find their value has grown to the point where you could reduce a significant portion of your debt simply by selling a few assets.

Drawing up a personal 'balance sheet' will give you a clearer picture of just where you stand. It is also something your lenders may want to see if you approach them to renegotiate your repayments (more on this later).

3. Prioritise your debts

Having drawn up your budget, you should have a better idea of how much of your income can be directed into paying off your debts. Different debts charge different rates of interest so it is important to prioritise your debts, taking the individual interest rates into account, so that they can be paid off more quickly.

Here's how you do it. List all the amounts that you owe by their interest rate rather than the balance. Put high-interest loans at the top of the list and work through all of your outstanding debts until the balances with the lowest rate are sitting at the bottom. Now, concentrate on paying off the debts that lie at the top of the list. You'll save more by paying off these expensive loans first, while keeping up the required repayments on the others.

If you have a number of debts around the same interest rate, pay off the smaller balances first. Knocking these off early will really make you feel like you're kicking some goals, giving you a good incentive to keep going.

There is a trick to paying off your debts this way, though. Let's say it costs you $50 each month to pay off the first debt. Once it is paid off, *add* that $50 to the minimum monthly payment on the second debt. Once this balance is paid off, add the total you were paying on that debt to the next one. In this way, as each debt is cleared, more and more can be used to pay off the next one, with the benefit that these payments are already built into your budget.

If you have both secured and unsecured loans, aim to pay off the unsecured balances first. Secured loans generally charge a lower interest rate, simply because the lender has a claim over one of your assets. The fact that the lender has some security also means they are usually more open to the idea of you reducing your repayments – at least until you've cleared the higher interest debts.

4. Pay more than the minimum

While it is tempting to build only the minimum debt repayments into your budget, it can be a recipe for disaster. This is because the minimum usually only just covers your interest, making very little impact on the principal.

To show you how this works, let's say that you took out a 20-year mortgage in January 2003 for $150 000 at 6.5% interest. The monthly repayments are $1118, but by January 2008 – a quarter of the way through the loan, and despite having repaid over $67 000 – you will still owe the bank over $128 000. That's a reduction in the principal of just $22 000.

The reason for this is that up until about halfway through the term, only a small proportion of every payment goes to paying off the outstanding balance. In the early days, the bulk of your repayments cover the interest which stays pretty much the same unless you make extra payments to reduce the principal. It's very much a case of taking one step forward and two steps backwards. On the flip side, any extra repayments you make will lower the principal, thereby reducing the interest, and the tide begins to turn in your favour.

A number of web sites have built-in calculators that can show you how much interest you will end up paying on a debt, how long it will take to pay off your credit card and other calculations that most of us would normally regard as incomprehensible. Two such web sites are www.bankchoice.com.au and www.bankrate.com, and they are well worth a look as they really drive home the point that sticking to the minimum repayments on a debt will see you paying the maximum interest bill.

5. Use up savings, if necessary

It may be a good idea to have a buffer of cash to cushion you from any unexpected hiccups, but it doesn't always make financial sense to save money in one hand when you are carrying big debts in the other.

The interest rate the bank pays on savings and deposits is much lower than the rate they charge on loans. After all, that's how they make their money. But income from savings accounts, term deposits and the like is fully taxable, which further reduces the return you are getting.

Consider this. A newlywed couple came to see me, looking for advice on how to save for their first home. They had $5000 in a term deposit earning 4.5% interest. That was a great start, but they also had a $10 000 personal loan, which they had used to pay for some of their wedding costs. The couple knew that it was probably better to use their savings to pay out the loan, but were concerned about having nothing to show for a few years in the workforce (other than memories of a darn good wedding day). So, they kept their loan repayments to a minimum and tried to put a bit away each month into their savings.

When we looked at the numbers, it was a strategy that just didn't stack up. The three-year loan was accruing interest of 11%. By the time it was paid off, the couple would have forked out $1800 in interest. They would have earned interest of $730 on their savings, but as they were both on the highest rate of tax, half of this would have gone to the tax man. The bottom line was that they were paying more *out* in interest than they were *earning in* interest.

So, instead, they used their savings to pay off part of the loan. By doing this they became debt-free in half the time, and they saved themselves $1400 in interest in the process. Having cleared themselves of debt, they could really focus on saving for a home.

6. Talk to your lenders

Lenders are in the business of receiving payments, and faced with the prospect of losing a debt altogether (if you go bankrupt), most creditors will accept a lower repayment. Talk to your creditors and tell them you're having difficulties – you will probably find they are open to revising your repayments and/or extending the time you have to pay.

Whatever you do, don't stop making repayments without warning. Nothing gets a creditor offside quicker. If you find your-self slipping into serious debt, do something about it sooner rather than later, and definitely well before you miss a payment. The best asset you have when you approach lenders to renegotiate your repayments is your past payment history, and creditors are far more likely to be co-operative if you have paid your bills on time up to this point.

When you approach your lenders, be as businesslike as possible. Make appointments to meet with your largest lenders, and instead of taking along an arsenal of sawn-off shotguns and a crowd of heavies from the local pub, bring a budget and a suggested repayment plan showing a specific amount allocated to each creditor. At the end of this book you will find a Debt Tracker, which is designed to help you keep on top of the amounts you owe, as well as noting any new repayments you have agreed on with your creditors. I cannot stress enough the importance of keeping a record of whom you have spoken to, and when, in your dealings with creditors. This way, if a dispute arises, you have a written record of what was agreed upon.

Among the solutions you can propose are a reduction in the principal, a reduction in the interest and/or an extension of time to repay. And if you have kept track of your spending you should be able to come up with a plan that is fair to your creditors and realistic for you.

If you don't feel comfortable dealing with creditors yourself, ask your accountant to act on your behalf. Alternatively, there are a number of non-profit financial counselling organisations that can work on your behalf, and a list of these is provided on page 93.

If a creditor is not willing to negotiate a new payment plan, the next step is to contact the Department of Fair Trading or Consumer Affairs in your state or territory. It may be possible to get a court order that sets out a new repayment schedule on the basis of hardship if you can show that:

- you have already tried to negotiate with your creditors
- your hardship is the result of unemployment, sickness or another reasonable cause, and
- your situation is likely to improve in the future.

Here's an incentive not to fall behind on your payments

You may think your tardiness is something known only to you and your lender, but nothing could be further from the truth.

Whenever you apply for credit, the lender will contact what's known as a 'credit bureau' or credit reporting service. These organisations hold records of everyone's credit history, keeping details of any loan defaults, court judgements made against you and even bounced cheques for a period of five years. So, any lapses in payment can certainly come back to haunt you.

They also record any applications you may have made to other credit providers as previous knock backs may mark you as a potential credit risk. For more information on how to take a look at your credit record, see Chapter 5.

Having agreed with your creditors on a new repayment plan, it is important to stick with it. Fall behind on your new repayments and your creditors are far less likely to have a sympathetic ear a second time around.

7. Consider consolidating your debts

Debt consolidation involves combining all your outstanding, higher-interest debts into one lower-interest loan. And in most cases, this means folding them into your mortgage. Consolidating high-interest personal loans and credit cards this way can be a sensible strategy which can more than halve the interest rate. But – and it's a big but – this strategy will only work if you break the spending habits that got you deep in hock in the first place.

You see, the downside to debt consolidation is that when you swap a higher-rate loan for one with a lower rate you generally extend the term of the debt, and that can mean more interest paid in the long run. It is like using your home loan to pay for consumer items and, unless you are financially disciplined, this can be crazy – you could still be paying for them decades later, long after they have well and truly gone.

If you fold a credit card debt into the home loan, for example, it will drag an otherwise short-term debt out over ten, 15 or even 20 years. For example, on a twenty-year mortgage of $120 000 at an interest rate of 6.5%, you would normally pay monthly payments of $894, with a total interest bill over the life of the loan of $94 725. Roll a $5000 credit card balance into the mortgage and your monthly repayments only rise by $40, but your total interest bill will escalate by about $4000 – meaning that over time you will have repaid $9000 on a debt of $5000. That's like paying the original card balance almost twice over!

The same applies to personal loans especially if there is only a short amount of the term left to run. It is often better just to hammer away at these loans for the time remaining, as consolidating them into your mortgage could see you end up paying interest on them for a lot longer.

This doesn't mean consolidation is not a worthwhile strategy – far from it. But there is no getting around the need to make as many additional payments as possible into your newly consolidated loan. Just because you now have one bigger low-interest loan does not mean you can sit back and take it easy. The creditors may have stopped queuing at your gate, but you've still got a big debt to pay and it's vital to pay it off as quickly as you possibly can.

The key to successfully consolidating your debts is sticking to a budget (there's just no escaping the importance of a budget in keeping your head above water), and when you approach a lender to consolidate your debts into one loan, the first thing you need to be able to show is that you can comfortably meet the new repayments. Remember, as a rule of thumb, creditors will want to see that your monthly debt repayments don't exceed 30% of your gross monthly income.

The second thing a lender will look for is security, which is why most debts are consolidated into your home loan. It is also the cheapest way to do it as mortgages generally carry the lowest rate of interest. But be aware that if the balance of your home loan rises above 80% of the value of your home, your lender will ask you to take out mortgage insurance, at your expense. This protects the lender, not you, in the event you can't make repayments.

If you don't have decent security like a residential property, or if your repayments chew up a big percentage of your income (more than 30% of your gross pay), you may well find you get the knock back from lenders when you ask about consolidating. If this happens to you, don't grab your credit card and head off for some morale-boosting retail therapy. Instead, give yourself three months to stick to your budget and chisel away at your debts. Then reapply to your bank, showing them that you can stick to a repayment plan.

How to consolidate your debts

1. *Be prepared when you approach your lender.* Any lender worth their salt will want to see a budget and a list of your assets and liabilities to establish your financial position.

2. *Write a proposal* outlining the loan(s) that you want to refinance and why.

3. *Approach your own lender first.* Demonstrate how a consolidation will help you meet your credit commitments. If your consolidation proposal gets the thumbs down, tell your bank manager you would like to revisit the application in, say, six months. This gives you the opportunity to prove you're able to stick to the repayments.

4. *Shop around* if you are not satisfied with your own bank's response.

5. *Once you have consolidated, revisit your budget* and make sure you are still making as many extra repayments as possible.

8. Cut up the cards and avoid debt triggers

One sure way to reduce the prospect of getting deep into debt is to remove the means of doing so, and that typically means cutting up your credit card (or cards). There is not much to be gained in going through the process of consolidating your debts into one loan if you go straight out and rack up more debts.

Credit cards are particularly hazardous for those who, by their own description, are 'born to shop'. 'Born to stay broke' is more like it. My recommendation to anyone who fits this description is to get rid of all your credit cards, *now*.

If you insist on keeping a credit card, limit it to just one (it is common for people with debt problems to have five or six), or, better still, use a debit card, which only draws cash from your bank account.

Just as budgeting will show you where you can cut back your spending, your monthly credit card statement will give you a good idea of where your spending weaknesses lie. Many people find that certain events trigger a spending binge. If the end-of-year sales are your idea of heaven, stay away from them. If impulse buying blows out your grocery bill, then learn to shop with a list, shop over the internet or get someone else to do the shopping, at least until you've reduced your debt.

9. Protect your income

Picture this. You are running around a footy field or a park with the kids when you slip and hurt your back. Suddenly, you are off work not just for a few days, but for weeks – possibly even months. Of course, we all think it will never happen to us, but if it does and you are left without an income for even a short period, you can find yourself being pushed to breaking point.

I realise that paying off large amounts of money doesn't leave you with a lot of surplus cash. But when you are carrying a lot of debt, income protection insurance is a must.

Before you take out a policy, check that you aren't already covered under an employer-sponsored superannuation scheme. For more on this, take a look at Chapter 10.

10. Seek professional help

Now, I am more than aware that sometimes debt can ensnare us no matter how hard we try to avoid it, through, say, our income unexpectedly drying up, an investment going bad or just rotten luck. Debt can put pressure on the remainder of the family finances and on the very fibre of the family itself. And if something's not done about it in a timely fashion, the consequences can be disastrous. It is under these circumstances that getting professional assistance and advice is very useful, if not essential.

You certainly don't have to wait until you are deep in debt before you approach a financial counsellor. Most counsellors give free or low-cost advice on many aspects of financial management, including budgeting. The Financial Counsellors Association of NSW's web site, which provides a list of contacts, is located at www.acwa.asn.au/fcan/. The following organisations can also help.

ACT – Care Financial Counselling Service (02) 6257 1788.

New South Wales – Wesley Mission Financial Counselling,
  c/- Credit Line 1800 808 488.

Victoria – Financial and Consumer Rights Council (03) 9663 2000.

Queensland – Financial Counsellors Services, Queensland
  (07) 3257 1957.

Western Australia – Consumer Credit Legal Service (08) 9481 7665.

South Australia – Community Legal Service (08) 8362 1199.

Tasmania – Anglicare Financial Counselling Service (03) 6223 4595.

Northern Territory – Anglicare Top End Financial Counselling Service
  (08) 8985 0000.

STAYING DEBT-FREE

Don't be flattered into taking on more debt

One thing that really irritates me about our financial institutions is their sometimes manic willingness to extend credit. Not that long ago, to get a loan you had to go cap-in-hand to a bank manager and show proof that you were in a position to service the loan. These days, it's almost the opposite.

Without any solicitation, people often receive letters inviting them to extend the limit on their credit card. For some people this is a bonus; for some a recipe for disaster. Someone who has already taken their card to the limit and is offered, say, an additional $1000 may initially think, 'What a windfall – some breathing space . . .' but, before long, the $1000 has gone, the minimum payment has increased and you're back in the never-never.

If you're offered an increased credit limit, the best thing to do may be to refuse it, unless you're in total control of your finances.

Don't take on someone else's debt

If someone said to you, 'Can I borrow your house – but you might not get it back', you'd tell them to go jump. Yet that is the sort of risk you take if you act as guarantor on someone else's loan.

Many people go guarantor on a loan for a loved one in the mistaken belief that it is just a formality to help them get credit. In fact, nothing could be further than the truth and agreeing to go guarantor is a big responsibility. You're not giving a character reference – you're agreeing to take over the debt or repay the full amount if the debtor does not or cannot repay it. And you could end up losing everything – even your home – if things go wrong.

The real rub is that if the person you're acting as guarantor for goes bankrupt, the creditors will start chasing you.

Before you agree to go guarantor for someone, take a good

look at the copy of the credit contract and if you have any doubts, maybe it's time to take your money – and possibly your affection – elsewhere.

Always remember cash is king

Let me lay my cards straight down on the table (and I don't mean my credit cards). If you want to buy something, try to pay cash or use lay-by. This is a simple, straightforward philosophy and, while it may not be practical for major purchases like a house or car, if you stick to it wherever possible, you shouldn't get into too much trouble with money or debt.

A FINAL WORD

Hopefully, this chapter has shown you how to bring your debt back to manageable levels and, just as importantly, how to keep it there. By now you're probably wondering when I'm going to talk about that other option for people burdened with debt – bankruptcy. I have deliberately avoided this issue until now because bankruptcy should be seen for what it is – an absolute last resort and not something to be entered into lightly. However, if you still find yourself sinking instead of swimming, turn to Chapter 5.

Beating bankruptcy

Sometimes you feel like you have it all. Then, when you least expect it, something happens out of the blue, and you lose everything – except, of course, your debts. Dealing with debt is stressful enough, but knowing that you could have difficulties paying it back is the stuff of nightmares. But, part of the fear of bankruptcy is that it's something many of us don't know too much about. And what we do know about it, most of us don't like.

There is no getting around the fact that bankruptcy is a black mark on your credit record – that's the track record of your ability to repay your debts. But for people struggling with overwhelming debts it can offer a much-needed fresh start, assuming that you choose to declare yourself bankrupt. Bear in mind, though, that your creditors (the people you owe money to) can also send you bankrupt. I'll be looking at how this can happen later on, but the end result is the same whether you go into bankruptcy voluntarily or not. First, though, let's take a look at what bankruptcy involves.

Bankruptcy is where a person, unable to pay his or her debts, agrees to give up control of their finances to a 'bankruptcy trustee', usually an accountant specialising in this area, in exchange for protection from creditors. Bankruptcies brought on by unemployment and consumer credit problems are on the rise, and in 2001/02 around 24 000 Australians were declared bankrupt.

I should point out that the term 'bankruptcy' only applies to people. So, if you are running a business as, say, a sole trader and the business can't pay its debts, *you* can be declared bankrupt. On the other hand, when a company can't meet its debts it is said to be 'insolvent', so instead of a bankruptcy trustee being appointed, a 'receiver' or 'administrator' may be brought in to sort the situation out.

In Chapter 4 I noted that for many people credit cards can be an express ticket to serious debt. If you ever needed convincing of this, take a look at long-term bankruptcy figures. The last 15 years have seen bankruptcies increase almost fourfold from around 7000 people nationally in 1986/87 to around 24 000 for the last couple of years. But, despite the relative ease with which you can declare yourself bankrupt, it's a step that should definitely be regarded as a last resort. It is estimated that every bankruptcy directly affects seven to ten other people, so it is well worth taking a look at the alternatives long before you embark on that road.

BANKRUPTCY MYTHS

When the creditors are lining up at your door, voluntary bankruptcy can seem like the best way out. But let's take a look at some of the 'myths' that surround bankruptcy, and once you've sorted out the fact from the fiction, it may not seem such an appealing alternative (assuming that you choose it – as opposed to having it inflicted upon you).

Possibly the biggest misconception is that bankruptcy clears all your debts. This is not necessarily the case. Some debts are *not* removed by bankruptcy, including outstanding child support, part of a Higher Education Contribution Scheme (HECS) debt, court-imposed fines or a Centrelink debt. These must still be paid.

More pressing for most people, though, is that creditors who have security over your property, such as a bank who holds a mortgage over your home, can sell the asset to recover the debt. And if you have asked someone (usually a friend or relative) to go guarantor on a loan, the creditor may start chasing them for the amount of the guarantee.

Declaring yourself bankrupt doesn't simply wipe the slate clean. If your annual take-home pay exceeds $33 442 (that's about $43 500 gross, indexed annually), half of every dollar you earn over this amount goes towards repaying your creditors (these payments are called 'contributions'). This threshold increases if you have dependents, but if you don't pay up, the trustee has the right to 'garnishee' from your pay packet (make deductions without your consent) or to extend your bankruptcy for longer than the standard three years (note that it is listed on your credit record or 'reference' for seven years).

As I noted above, when you are declared bankrupt, a bankruptcy trustee is appointed to take control of your financial affairs. The majority of your assets become the property of your bankruptcy trustee, who is expected to sell them and distribute the proceeds among your creditors. So, if you come good during your period of bankruptcy, either by winning the lottery or inheriting some money, this too can be used to pay off your creditors. Not that your chances of winning a lottery are all that good, as you can be prosecuted for contributing to your bankruptcy through gambling or speculation.

As a bankrupt, you face some serious limitations. You'll need the permission of your trustee or the court if you want to travel overseas. You can't be a director or manager of a company, and while you can still operate a business, you'll need to disclose your status as a bankrupt to anyone you have dealings with – hardly the sort of information that is good for business.

Bankruptcy also does you no favours in terms of your credit rating. Most people reaching the stage where they are seriously considering bankruptcy probably have a less than perfect credit record, usually the result of lenders reporting payment defaults. But, while your bankruptcy may stay on your credit rating for seven years, it is recorded *permanently* on what's known as the National Personal Insolvency Index. This is a database maintained by the Insolvency and Trustee Service Australia (ITSA), the government-owned bankruptcy trustee service. And this database is publicly accessible. For a small fee anyone can look up to see whether or not you are, or have been, a bankrupt.

Apart from the lingering social stigma, it can have other consequences, including seriously affecting your employment opportunities if you work in a job handling money, in the security industry, in many professions or as a licensed builder. It can be hard to rent a home or obtain phone or electricity connections without a bond, and you face the humiliation of having to declare your status as a bankrupt if you make a purchase on credit or by cheque if the amount is over $3900 (this amount is indexed annually).

So, while voluntary bankruptcy may appear to be a way out of your debts, it has some serious downsides and you can't simply change your mind once you have declared yourself bankrupt. In addition, the government has recently cracked down on the bankruptcy system. These changes are discussed in more detail on page 109, but be aware that the system is being made more rigorous. With this in mind I urge you to read on and find out what your options are, but it is worth stressing that the important thing is to take action well before bankruptcy becomes the only option.

ALTERNATIVES TO BANKRUPTCY

Informal agreements

If you find yourself facing financial difficulties, bite the bullet and get in touch with your creditors before a payment is missed. Nothing gets a lender's back up more quickly than missed repayments. But, most creditors, given advance notice, will offer an extension of time, or a schedule of smaller repayments, in preference to writing off the debt altogether. You can find a Debt Tracker at the end of this book, which is designed to help you keep track of what you owe and to record any new repayment arrangements.

The downside, for you, of these informal arrangements is that they are not binding on your creditors. They can still take action at any time to make you pay in full.

If you feel uncomfortable about approaching a creditor yourself, a financial counsellor or an accountant can act on your behalf. Some of the agencies that can help are listed towards the end of Chapter 4.

Formal arrangements

The law surrounding personal bankruptcy is set out in the federal Bankruptcy Act, which, like a lot of legislation, is numbered in roman numerals – V for five, IX for nine, and so on. So, if you were having a conversation about a 'Part X Arrangement', you would call it a 'Part Ten' arrangement, because that's the section of the Bankruptcy Act that it comes from.

Debt agreements (known as Part IX or 'Part Nine' agreements)

Debt agreements were introduced in 1996 as an alternative to bankruptcy for people on low incomes with relatively small debts, so they are not open to everyone. A debt agreement is available to you where your unsecured debts (amounts you owe to a creditor who has no claim over any of your property) and your assets are each worth less than $66 885 and your after-tax income is below $33 442 (both these figures are indexed periodically for inflation).

When you enter into a debt agreement, you make a collective offer to your creditors, setting out a suggested repayment plan that meets your ability to pay and which will hopefully keep your creditors happy. You can suggest an instalment plan, payment in a lump sum, or offer an asset to 'swap' for the debt. But the proposal must be made through ITSA (see page 110). Your accountant or an ITSA representative handles the payment schedule, and your creditors must respond in writing to accept or reject the proposal. If the proposal is accepted, it is legally binding.

Here's how it works. Let's say you have total debts of $5000, your annual income is $20 000 and you have no assets of any significant value. If you were made bankrupt, it is unlikely that your creditors would receive anything as your income is below the level where they are entitled to half your earnings. So, most creditors would be better off accepting a debt agreement. You draft a proposal to pay each of your creditors, say, $100 a month (or whatever you feel you can comfortably manage), and you show the proposal to ITSA.

If ITSA thinks the repayment plan is reasonable, they will put the offer to each of your creditors, who then have 25 days to respond. During this time, none of your assets can be repossessed and no one can garnishee your wages. If the majority of your creditors accept your proposal, the debt agreement becomes legally binding on all your creditors, regardless of whether they are happy with the agreement, or even if they didn't respond to it. You then send the money to ITSA and they distribute it to your creditors for you.

The advantage of using a debt agreement is that it is you (and not your creditors) who decides the terms of the offer, so your proposed repayments can be tailored to whatever you feel comfortable with. It's an option worth looking into, but there are restrictions. Even if you meet the income limits, you can't use a debt agreement if in the last decade you have already been bankrupt, have had a previous debt agreement or have entered a Part X arrangement (see below).

Part X or 'Part Ten' debt arrangements

No income, debt or asset limits apply with Part X (Ten) arrangements and the basic difference from a Part IX debt agreement is that you hire a private trustee to act as a go-between with your creditors, rather than going through ITSA. You must appoint a solicitor or trustee to take control of your financial affairs and, after meeting with your creditors, an arrangement is worked out on how to best settle your debts. While many creditors will agree to a proposed repayment plan, they certainly don't have to. They can request that you bankrupt yourself, and if you refuse they are entitled to apply to the Federal Court to have you made a bankrupt.

Note, though, that your solicitor or trustee will want to be paid for their services, which involves drawing up a repayment schedule and meeting with creditors. These services do not come cheaply, and you could end up paying around $5000 to cover the fees that will be racked up clinching a Part X arrangement, which is why many people simply opt for bankruptcy.

BANKRUPTCY

Voluntary bankruptcy

Anyone can voluntarily declare themselves bankrupt, regardless of how much they owe. The first step is known as 'presenting a declaration of intention to lodge a debtor's petition'. In plain English, this simply means giving ITSA notice that you intend to declare yourself bankrupt. Once you've lodged your declaration, you have a seven-day cooling off period during which your creditors can't take any action against you. This will give you temporary relief from your creditors, but don't look on it as a handy stalling technique, as you can only lodge a declaration of intention once in any 12-month period.

If your petition passes muster with ITSA, and you still want to proceed after seven days, you need to fill in two forms, a 'debtor's petition' in which you declare yourself bankrupt, and a 'statement of affairs' setting out your income, your assets and all the details of your debts. Both are available from ITSA, financial counsellors or registered bankruptcy trustees. Once the forms are accepted by ITSA, you are officially bankrupt.

I mentioned earlier, on page 99, that the bankruptcy system is undergoing a number of changes which, at the time of writing in early 2003, are scheduled for introduction in May 2003. One of these changes is that ITSA will have the power to reject a debtor's petition if it looks like the applicant really can pay their debts, but is just trying to give their creditors the slip.

Involuntary bankruptcy

A creditor can apply to have you declared bankrupt where your outstanding debts total just $2000 or more. It's not a great deal of money to be made bankrupt over, but it won't happen overnight. It tends to be a fairly lengthy process – far longer than it takes to become bankrupt voluntarily, as there is a reasonable amount of going back and forth to court to resolve various issues.

Secured creditors (those with a right to one or more of your assets if you default on the loan) have the right to take possession of the particular piece of property if you fall behind in your payments. The procedure they use to go about this very much depends on the state in which you live and the terms of the contract.

On the other hand, unsecured creditors don't have the luxury of being able to seize any of your assets if you fail to make good on the debt. Instead, they have to take a 'creditor's petition' to the court, which is basically a request for the court to declare you bankrupt. There's no doubt that it's all pretty stern stuff but, as a rule, unsecured creditors will only tip you into bankruptcy as a last resort. Unless you own valuable assets, they don't stand to get much anyway, and if you are made bankrupt at the request of a creditor it is they, not you, who could end up paying the associated legal bills.

What does bankruptcy involve?

Once you are declared bankrupt, a bankruptcy trustee takes control of your financial affairs. In practice, this means selling your assets – including possibly your home – to pay creditors. Your unsecured creditors cannot take any further action. Secured creditors can recover the asset over which they have a claim, and sell it.

Some of your assets are protected and can't be sold. This includes household furniture, clothing and your super. Also protected is a vehicle valued up to $5650 and tools of trade worth up to $2850 (these amounts are indexed annually). Remember, too, that your trustee may take any assets you build up after becoming bankrupt.

How long will I be bankrupt for?

The normal period for bankruptcy is three years, but it can be extended to five or even eight years if you commit offences under the Bankruptcy Act. This includes applying for credit without informing the lender that you are an undischarged bankrupt.

As at April 2003, it is possible to have your bankruptcy discharged early, and around a third of bankruptcies only last six months. To be eligible, you will need to meet a range of conditions set out in the Bankruptcy Act, including the requirement that your debts total less than 150% of your pre-bankruptcy income.

Any time during the bankruptcy you can draw up a schedule of proposed payments for your creditors. If it is accepted by the majority of your creditors, the proposal (known as a 'Section 73 proposal') can be accepted and your bankruptcy annulled. There is no obligation on your creditors to accept such an arrangement, but there are times when bankruptcy prevents you from earning an income (for example, bankruptcy prevents accountants from practising), so by annulling your bankruptcy, your chances of earning an income are higher and your creditors stand a better chance of being repaid.

It is worth pointing out that the threefold increase in bankruptcies over the last 15 years has not escaped the attention of our policy makers. While the easy availability of credit (especially that old culprit, credit cards) has pushed a lot of genuine battlers into bankruptcy, it is an option being chosen by some people for reasons other than financial failure. In some instances, people are declaring themselves bankrupt to avoid Family Court settlements, or over ridiculously small debts. The result is that changes are being proposed that will make it harder to declare yourself bankrupt and to get an early discharge.

At the time of writing, it is anticipated that in May 2003 the option of early discharge from bankruptcy will be abolished, and all bankruptcies will run for the full three years. On the flipside, in an attempt to encourage people with financial difficulties to use debt agreements, the after-tax income threshold for these Part IX (Nine) agreements is set to be raised from $33 442 to $46 800.

So when is bankruptcy a reasonable option?

Bankruptcy should be the last resort for everyone. But under extreme circumstances those people who have the least to lose from bankruptcy are those who:

- have overwhelming debts that they could not repay within three years (the standard period of bankruptcy), *and*
- whose annual take-home pay is less than $33 442 (indexed), *and*

- who own few or no assets of value, *and*
- who are unlikely to need credit for seven years (the time bankruptcy sits on your credit record).

This certainly narrows it down to a very thin slice of the population, and unless this describes your situation, I urge you to give serious thought to the implications of voluntary bankruptcy before you go ahead.

Bankruptcy does not generally affect your superannuation entitlements. There are two exceptions to this. The first is where your super exceeds the current Reasonable Benefits Limit, which for most of us is $1 124 384. The second is pension payments made from your super savings providing income over the bankruptcy limit of $33 442.

LIFE AFTER BANKRUPTCY

Bankruptcy can be an enormous relief to people who are experiencing genuine financial distress. Your bankruptcy trustee handles all claims, so declaring yourself bankrupt generally gets the creditors off your doorstep. The problem is that you're left with a lingering record, which can be a serious stumbling block when you apply for a loan in the future.

Whenever you approach a lender they will want to review your credit record. This shows any black marks against your name, including any loan defaults (missed payments), rejections for credit by other lenders and, of course, any bankruptcies. Each item on your credit record is dated, and after five years items are automatically deleted – except for bankruptcy, which stays there for seven years. Not surprisingly, catching sight of 'bankruptcy' on a credit record sends most lenders diving for cover.

The passing of time and a good repayment history are the best means of wiping the slate clean – but it's a chicken-and-egg situation. Re-establishing a good credit record is hard because no one will lend to you on the basis of your past problems.

Now, I am certainly not suggesting that you rush out and get back into hock as soon as your bankruptcy is discharged, but the fact is that there are some things in life that we need finance to buy – a home being the obvious example. The good news, though, is that in addition to the growing number of alternative lenders who will lend to a discharged bankrupt, there are ways to improve your credit rating.

The first thing to do is get hold of your own credit record to see what sort of information lenders would be likely to see about you (see 'What lenders read about you' on page 108). If some of the records are approaching five years, it could be worth postponing your application for credit until the offending item has been automatically deleted. If you have had debt problems but have tried hard to fix them, you can contact Baycorp Advantage (phone (02) 9464 6000), one of Australia's largest credit bureaus, and ask to have this noted on your file.

The best way around the problem, though, is to develop a savings record to counteract your credit record. Bankrupts are entitled to earn an income, although do bear in mind once your after-tax income exceeds $33 442 you will have to pay contributions to your creditors. But bankrupts are *not* supposed to build assets. So, the best course of action may be to use your bankruptcy to save whatever you can. You are entitled to keep what you earn, so if you build up some savings in three years of bankruptcy, it can be used to show banks and credit unions that while you have had a few tough years in the past, you now have an established savings pattern. However, this is an area where you need to take care. The distinction between what is an 'asset' and what is 'unspent income' is not entirely clear and it is easy to unknowingly put your money into something that can be repossessed by your bankruptcy trustee for distribution among your creditors. Building up savings from your income is something you should discuss with your trustee, but your safest bet may be to leave any savings in an everyday bank account. Invest the money in something like, say, shares, and it becomes an asset that can be handed over to your creditors.

What lenders read about you

Baycorp Advantage is one of Australia's largest credit bureaus, maintaining the credit records of millions of Australians for review by commercial lenders. To get a copy of your credit rating, you'll need to send the following details to Baycorp Advantage Public Inquiries, PO Box 964, North Sydney NSW, 2059:

- your full name
- your date of birth
- your driver's licence number
- your address and phone number.

It's a free service.

Alternative lenders

There was a time when anyone with a few dents in their credit record could forget about getting a home loan. Thankfully, those days are over, and while bankruptcy should be a last resort, there's no reason why most of us should be branded for life by past financial problems.

The rising number of personal bankruptcies has created a new market for so-called 'non-conforming' lenders, who are prepared to lend to applicants who don't fit mainstream lending criteria.

These lenders, like GE Mortgage Solutions and Liberty Financial, now account for around 10% of the mortgage market.

The catch is, to be eligible you may need to provide a large deposit (around 15% of the property's purchase price) and an interest rate higher than that of the major banks may be charged, reflecting the greater risk for the lender.

The good news with these loans is that after one or two years many borrowers are able to refinance with a traditional lender offering lower interest rates. This is because by then the borrowers have re-established a good credit record and a steady income history with the alternative lender. However, some non-conforming lenders, realising they may lose part of their business after a few years, charge hefty early repayment fees. These fees may be sufficiently high to deter people from refinancing, so be sure to ask about early repayment charges before you sign up for the loan, as they are usually buried in the small print.

Proposed changes to bankruptcy laws

I've already mentioned that a number of changes to bankruptcy laws are due to take place in May 2003. These changes have been introduced in response to concerns that bankruptcy is seen as an easy way out that favours debtors over creditors. And while the vast majority of people who become bankrupt are genuine battlers, there has also been an increase in the number of people turning to bankruptcy more than once. For example, in 2001/02, more than one in ten bankrupts had been declared bankrupt at least once before.

The changes to bankruptcy law are designed to make the alternatives to bankruptcy more accessible while making bankruptcy itself less appealing. The major changes include:

- Getting rid of the early discharge option and making all bankruptcies last for at least three years. This term can be extended if the bankrupt doesn't co-operate with their trustee.

- A debtor's petition can be rejected if it looks as though the bankrupt really could pay their debts, but is just looking for an easy way out.
- Debt agreements are being made more accessible, with the after-tax income limit for Part IX agreements being raised to $46 800 (at the time of writing, no changes to the asset or liability limits for these agreements had been mentioned).

For more information on bankruptcy and its alternatives, contact the Insolvency and Trustee Service Australia (www.itsa.gov.au):

Adelaide: 08 8112 4300

Brisbane: 07 3360 5444

Canberra: 02 6270 3600

Darwin: 08 8980 2000 (Note: the Darwin office closed in mid-2002, but enquiries are redirected to the Adelaide office on this telephone number for the cost of a local call.)

Hobart: 03 6221 7777

Melbourne: 03 9272 4800

Perth: 08 9268 1222

Sydney: 02 8233 7800

6

Surviving redundancy and unemployment

How the world of work has changed! Just a generation or two ago, we left school at either 16 or 18, landed a job with no trouble at all and retired around 40 or so years later – often from the same company that hired us initially. Full-time work was regarded as the norm, and for my dad's generation, almost half the workforce was employed in industry and manufacturing.

It's a radically different picture these days. Take a look at some of the new words we use, like 'privatisation', 'globalisation' and 'outsourcing', and you begin to get the picture. On average, we change jobs every three to four years, a good number of us work for ourselves, and an increasingly large proportion of the unemployed – nearly 25% – have been out of work for over a year. Whether you call it 'restructuring', 'downsizing', or plain old 'bankruptcy', the workplace my dad's generation knew, with its job security and job stability, has gone the way of the dinosaur.

But, it's not all bad news. In February 2003, the unemployment rate was 6%, down from a high of almost 11% ten years ago. So how has unemployment fallen, despite all this upheaval on the job scene? The answer lies in the new industries that have developed to fill the gap. And the only sure way of gaining a firm footing in the shifting sands of the job market is to chase a career in one of these growing areas of the economy. There are certainly job opportunities around, but before trying to figure out where they are, let's look at the more pressing issue of where redundancy or retrenchment is likely to leave you in the short term. I should point out that I'll stick with the term 'redundancy' for the sake of simplicity.

BEING MADE REDUNDANT

Technically speaking, 'redundancy' occurs when an employer simply does not want a job performed any more, be it the result of a restructure, the closure of a business or the introduction of new technology. And I reckon every one of us would know someone who has been made redundant or experienced a period of unemployment over the last decade. In fact, in recent years, the collapse of household names like Ansett, HIH Insurance and One.Tel has begun to make the business sector look more like a war zone. And it is easy for Australians to believe that the prospects of being made redundant are probably greater than ever.

But despite all the corporate upheavals, the rate of redundancies has actually remained fairly constant over the past two decades. Even in the good years, the Australian Bureau of Statistics (ABS) has recorded a redundancy rate of around 4% of the workforce. It makes redundancy our single biggest cause of unemployment, and 3.3 million Australians over the last decade alone would argue that these days none of us are safe from the dreaded tap on the shoulder.

Thankfully, redundancy no longer carries the stigma it used to, and whether yours is a forced or voluntary redundancy, the majority of people who've been through the experience say it was a major turning point in their lives, and often one for the better – although it may not always feel that way at the time.

Voluntary redundancy

'Voluntary' redundancy packages, where you put your hand up to be made redundant, often seem like a pretty good deal at first glance. After all, how many times in your life are you offered a few thousand dollars to stay *away* from work? But don't be tempted to grab the money on offer without plenty of thought and planning. The payment being dangled in front of you may sound like a lot, but unless you are confident of finding a new job quickly, the money might have to stretch a lot further than you first thought.

In voluntary redundancies, your employer, keen to see staff numbers drop, may be more generous than in a forced redundancy. And if acceptance of the offer is slow, you might be able to negotiate your own package. But it can be something of a cat and mouse game, as an employer facing few, if any, acceptances might just replace the voluntary redundancies with a less generous round of forced retrenchments.

When your employer goes belly up

Losing your job when the business has gone bust is quite different from being retrenched from an otherwise healthy business.

When a business goes down the tube, it is the secured creditors (those with a claim over one or more assets) who are at the top of the financial pecking order. Employees are entitled to be paid for any annual leave and long service leave owing to them as well as any unpaid wages, but when a company is insolvent (or the owner of a business goes bankrupt), there may not be enough money to go around.

Enter the government-funded General Employee Entitlements and Redundancy Scheme (GEERS). Set up in 2001, this scheme is designed to compensate employees for their various salary entitlements if their employer has become insolvent or bankrupt. Under GEERS, you can claim for unpaid wages and annual or long service leave, as well as up to eight weeks' redundancy pay. The benefits are paid to a maximum annual income of $81 500 (for 2002/03), so if your salary was higher you may still be eligible for GEERS, but you'll be paid as if you were earning $81 500. For more information on this, contact the Department of Employment and Workplace Relations on 1300 135 040.

Whether your redundancy is forced or voluntary, it is likely to raise plenty of emotional issues as well as concerns over money – concerns you probably thought, or at least hoped, you would never have to deal with. And for most people going through the redundancy wringer, the most pressing concerns are 'What should I do with the payout?' and 'How do I get another job?' I'll look at getting back into the workforce a bit later, but first let's tackle the money matters.

TAKE STOCK OF YOUR FINANCES
Your redundancy payout
The payout you receive is usually made up of several parts, each of which is taxed separately. In general, a redundancy payout comprises:

1. any unused annual leave and long service leave
2. termination pay – also known as 'severance pay', and
3. your superannuation.

1. Unused annual leave and long service leave
If you have any unused holiday pay owing to you, it will be paid to you as a lump sum and is taxable up to a maximum rate of

31.5%. If your marginal tax rate (the top rate of tax you pay) is below 31.5%, you will be taxed at the lower rate. Any unused long service leave pay is also generally taxed at a maximum rate of 31.5%.

2. Termination pay

Your termination pay is a sum of money designed to soften the blow of losing your job. It's often measured as a number of weeks of pay, but the amount you are paid is largely up to your employer. It will depend on things like how long you've been in the job, the industry you work in, as well as your position and salary at the time of being retrenched. If you're employed under an award or enterprise agreement, the award will spell out the minimum payment you're entitled to.

Despite the cost involved in making redundancies, big organisations are often keen to part with their staff on good terms. This is partly because large-scale redundancies can tarnish their public image, but also because it can lower the morale of the (understandably concerned) remaining staff. So, redundancy packages are often quite generous, and payments typically comprise four weeks' pay, plus an extra two weeks' pay for each year of service. So, for example, if you have been in your job for 12 years on a salary of $800 per week (before tax), your termination pay could be around $22 400 ($800 × 4 + $800 × 2 × 12).

Part of your termination payment, known as a 'bona fide' redundancy payment, will be tax-free. You get the first $5623 tax-free, plus a further $2812 is tax-free for each complete year of service (these amounts are indexed each year). So, if you have been in your job for six years, the tax-free component of your redundancy payout would be $22 495 ($5623 + $2812 × 6).

This amount cannot be rolled over (paid directly) into a super fund, but you can use it to make an additional contribution to your super. If you do this, it will be classified as an 'undeducted contribution', meaning you haven't had any tax breaks on it, but it will be 'preserved' – that is, you won't be able to withdraw it from the fund until age 55, and only then if you retire. Note, too, that anyone aged under 42 years has a higher preservation age.

The balance of your redundancy payout (excluding super-annuation) is called an 'eligible termination payment' (ETP). This is where it starts to get interesting, because the amount of tax you pay on the ETP will depend on what you do with it – and you don't have long to decide. For ETPs over $5000, it's compulsory for your employer to give you an ETP 'pre-payment statement', setting out the amount that you're entitled to. You've then got 30 days to let your employer know whether you want to take the ETP in cash, roll it over into a super fund, or rollover part of it and take the rest as cash. If you opt to take an amount as cash, you can't change your mind and roll it over into your super fund later.

As a rule, under-55s pay more tax on their ETP if they choose to take the payment as cash rather than rolling it over. This is designed to encourage us to build up a super nest egg to help pay for our retirement. I'll take a closer look at this issue shortly, but when you are deciding how to take the ETP, you need to weigh up your need for cash in the short term, against the tax savings to be had by putting the money into super for the long term.

If you have been with your employer for a long time, your ETP may be divided into two parts – the part that relates to your employment pre-July 1983, and the part relating to post-June 1983.

Pre-July 1983 ETP You'll pay no tax if you roll this part of the payout into a super fund. If you take it as cash, 95% of the amount is tax-free and the remaining 5% goes into your tax return to be taxed at your normal rate.

Post-June 1983 ETP If you rollover this amount into your super, it will be taxed at 15%. If you take it as cash, the tax you pay will depend on your age. If you're over 55, the first $112 405 (for 2002/03) is taxed at 16.5%, with the balance taxed at 31.5%. Under-55s are taxed at a maximum rate of 31.5%.

Let's take a look at how it works. We'll say, for example, that Alexander (aged 37) was retrenched from his job of five years in December 2002. He had no unused annual or long service leave, but his employer gave him a redundancy payout of $40 000. Alexander felt uncertain about his prospects of getting another job soon, so he opted to receive the full amount in cash. Here's how his payout will be taxed:

Alexander's redundancy payout	$40 000
His tax-free amount – this is his bona fide redundancy payment comprised of $5623 plus $2812 × 5 (as explained on page 115).	$19 683
The balance remaining is Alexander's taxable ETP	$20 317
The pre-July 1983 amount is nil because Alexander has only worked for his current employer for five years	–
Post-July 1983 amount	$20 317
Tax payable ($20 317 × 31.5%)	**$ 6 400**
As Alexander is aged under 55, he will pay a maximum rate of tax (plus Medicare) on his taxable ETP of 31.5%.	
Balance of ETP after tax ($20 317 less $6400)	$13 917
Plus: tax-free bona fide redundancy payment	$19 683
Net (after-tax) amount received by Alexander	**$33 600**

So, out of a total redundancy pay of $40 000, Alexander will receive $33 600 (being $19 683 + $13 917). If he chose to rollover the lot into a super fund, he would halve the taxman's cut to $3047 ($20 317 × 15%), but the catch is that he can't access this money until he retires. If he was older and closer to retirement, he may well opt to roll the lot over.

Now, as if taxing people who've lost their job isn't bad enough, a 'superannuation surcharge' may also be payable on ETPs. This will only affect you if what's called your 'adjusted taxable income' (don't ask) is over the threshold of $90 527 (indexed) and it is only levied on that part of your payout that relates to service since August 1996. The surcharge starts at 1%, rising to 15% when your income hits $109 924. This income might sound high, but it can often be easy for an ETP to push you over the line. This additional impost is enormously complicated and don't attempt to tackle it without a stiff drink on hand. However, the bottom line is that you will pay more in tax if you take your ETP as cash rather than rolling it over into your super.

Unless you need the money, it can make sense to roll it over into a super fund. After all, why pay 31.5% tax when you can avoid it, simply by rolling it over? However, unless your job prospects are good, or you are close to retiring, you may need more cash to live on than you realise. My advice here is to get some professional guidance during the month or so that you have to decide how you want the payment to be made. Good advice will cost you, but the fact is that ETPs can be a tax minefield, and without some decent help you could end up paying a lot more to the taxman than you might to a financial adviser or accountant.

One factor which may affect your decision to roll an ETP into your super is the much-maligned 'Reasonable Benefits Limit' (RBL). This is the maximum amount you can have in super-annuation before you get hit with some very hefty tax penalties. The RBL varies according to how your super is paid out come retirement, and for the financial year ending June 2003, the RBL for lump sums is $562 195. If you opt to have a substantial part of your super paid out as a pension (a series of regular payments a bit like the wage of your working days), the RBL is $1 124 384. Any amount you have above these levels (which are adjusted annu-ally for wage rises) is called an 'excess benefit' and these are taxed at the highest marginal rate of tax, plus the Medicare levy. So you could end up paying 48.5% in tax on the excess. I mention this here despite the fact that very few of us will ever have to worry about the 'problem' of excess super.

If you need further information on ETPs and super rollovers, the Tax Office can be contacted on 131 020. They can let you know how much tax you'll be up for but they cannot give you any financial planning advice – for this you'll need to talk to your accountant or financial adviser.

When you reach a decision on how you want to take your ETP, put it in writing, giving one copy to your employer and keeping a copy for yourself (the Tax Office requires you to keep this written authorisation for five years). If, for whatever reason, you receive a payout in cash without any prior notice from your employer, you've got seven days to rollover your ETP into a super fund. After this, super funds need written permission from the Tax Office before they can accept the rollover.

3. Your superannuation entitlements

You may also be entitled to some super if you are made redundant. Some of this money, if it relates to pre-July 1999, may be a 'non-preserved benefit' and you may opt to withdraw this amount. (Your 'statement of termination payment' will tell you what your payment is comprised of.) However, it is likely that most of your money will be 'preserved', which means that the money must remain in the super system until you turn 55. This doesn't mean you have to keep the money in your current super fund, though, and if you are a member of an employer-sponsored fund, you will have to find a new home for your nest egg, and a decent financial planner can advise you on which super fund is best suited to your particular circumstances.

There is no doubt that anyone going through the enormously stressful experience of redundancy and unemployment would want to draw on their super nest egg. However, super is designed to provide your retirement income, and to keep it for that purpose, the government has put in place some very tight restrictions on when you can withdraw your super prior to retirement. Any 'non-preserved' amounts you have in super – generally those that relate to the period before July 1999 – may be accessible, and your super fund can advise you of these. However, all super contributions plus the fund's earnings since July 1999 (and that includes any you choose to make from your after-tax income) are 'preserved' and must remain in the super system until you retire and are aged 55 or older. (This age limit is being increased gradually so that by 2025 it will be age 60 for those people born after June 1964.)

I look at how you can get early access to your super in more detail in Chapter 10, but as a rule you can only get your hands on the preserved part of your super if you are experiencing extreme financial hardship, or on the grounds of compassion. For more information, you can contact your super fund or the Australian Prudential Regulation Authority (APRA) on 1300 131 060.

Having said that, I reckon your best bet is to leave your super until you retire. I realise that for many Australians redundancy and unemployment can be a very tough time when your finances can be really squeezed, but hopefully your circumstances will change for the better, and the super you leave untouched today will continue to grow and accumulate until the day you choose to exit the workforce. And, bear in mind that further down the track you could have 20 years or more of retirement to provide for.

Accessing your super early may keep the wolves from the door, but regard it as a last resort. Rather than focusing on how to get access to your retirement nest egg, concentrate on managing the money you have now, and focus your efforts on getting back into the workforce – and that's what I'll look at next.

SURVIVING FINANCIALLY

Redundancy often comes with a great deal of uncertainty. Issues like what you should do with the payout and where (and when) your next pay packet will come from, are all perfectly understandable concerns. However, once you've worked out how much of your redundancy pay you'll keep as cash, the only hard and fast rule that follows is to think first and spend later.

The money might be needed for day-to-day living, or even to start up a new business venture, so you need to give yourself time to think. Don't put the money in an everyday savings account – it will earn next to nothing in interest and it's a strategy that will make your bank rich and you poor. The first step is to park your funds in a well-paying account like a cash management trust, where it can safely earn around 4%. This will also give you some breathing space while you decide how to invest for the long term, while looking at your career options.

Unless you have a new job lined up, you need to remain as financially flexible as possible. So don't tie up your money by paying off debts or buying investments. Paying down your mortgage or personal loans are steps that I'd normally applaud, but this could leave you strapped for cash further down the track unless you land another job fairly quickly.

The next step is to plan your finances to see you through to re-employment. The only way to do this is with a budget, and you'll find a Budget Planner at the end of this book, which is designed to make the process a bit easier. Now, I realise that the thought of doing a budget probably doesn't set your pulse racing, but it really is essential if your income has dropped.

Drawing up a budget as soon as your income changes will help you to:

- take care of your *needs* before your *wants*
- match your spending levels to your changed income

- make better decisions about spending your money, and
- avoid or help resolve any family disputes over money.

The budget you use during a period of unemployment will probably be a bit different from your normal budget. It's likely you'll be less certain about how much money is coming in, so you really need to have a good idea of where the money is going out.

The first step is to calculate your monthly income, making sure you include any government entitlements (more on this later). Next, work out your monthly expenses. If you have always used a budget you will have a reasonable idea of your monthly spending patterns. But bear in mind that on a reduced income you will need to plan your spending more, so look for luxury or unnecessary expenses that you could cut out fairly painlessly. Next, balance your income with your expenses. This may be difficult, but it is important to stay within your income.

If your money is going out faster than it is coming in, you have several options.

- *Cut back on your expenses.* With your wallet a bit leaner, each spending decision becomes more important. Buy cheaper items instead of the more expensive ones, see if the purchase is something you can share or even exchange with friends or neighbours and, most importantly, ask yourself if you really need the item.
- *Increase your income through part-time work, temp jobs or consulting.*
- *Make better use of your assets.* Look at your assets to see if there is anything that could be used (or even sold) to help bring in extra cash.
- *Reduce your fixed payments by speaking with your creditors* (for more on this take a look at Chapter 4).

Make your budget work

Having drawn up a budget, here's one way to make it work. Your budget will tell you how much it costs you and your family to live each month. We'll call this amount your 'living allowance'. Whenever you receive any income (be it from government entitlements, part-time work or whatever), deposit it into your everyday bank account, and hold onto each month's living allowance – think of it as 'paying yourself'. Anything left over in the account should be transferred to an interest-bearing account (an online savings account will give you a good rate of interest with your money at call) and kept for emergencies. Hopefully you'll land another job before you need it, but it's always reassuring to know it's there.

Government financial support

There are a number of government support systems to help see you through to re-employment and it is a good idea to register for Centrelink benefits as early as possible – even if you think your chances of snaring another job quickly are high. If you are under 21 and looking for a job, you may be eligible for Youth Allowance (see Chapter 2). The rest of us who are too young for the age pension may be entitled to Newstart Allowance. The rate is around $380 per fortnight (indexed twice a year) and you may also be entitled to some rent assistance, although families with children sometimes receive this as part of their Family Tax Benefit (see Chapter 3).

Newstart is both income and assets tested. For example, you can earn up to $62 each fortnight before Centrelink cuts back your allowance. Tables showing the Newstart income and assets limits are found at the end of this chapter.

TAKE STOCK OF YOUR OPTIONS

Look, there's no doubt redundancy can put you through the emotional wringer, but if correctly handled it can provide an unexpected sea change in life. Once you have the financial side of things under control, the trick to getting through what can be a stressful time is to remain flexible. Don't go looking for that elusive job for life – statistics show that such a thing doesn't exist any more.

Just ask Martine Richards, who wrote to me for advice after being made redundant. A former flight attendant, Martine was one of 17 000 Ansett staff who suddenly found themselves out of a job when the airline collapsed in 2001.

Although Martine wasn't altogether surprised by the announcement that the airline had folded, the news still came as a shock. It was a job she put her heart and soul into, yet she was left with nothing to show for it – through no fault of her own.

But, like a lot of people who've been down the redundancy road, the airline's demise has opened the way for a new career path for Martine. The fact is Martine has alopecia, a condition that leaves sufferers with no hair. And using her expertise in this area, Martine has set up her own business – 'Freedom Wigs Australia', which imports custom-made wigs.

Even though Martine has hands-on knowledge, starting out in any new business is risky. But one little-known support system for people getting through redundancy is the option of claiming benefits for retraining through the New Enterprise Incentive Scheme (NEIS).

The scheme is pitched at helping people who are setting up their own business. You get ongoing business advice, training in putting together a business plan and financial assistance. The NEIS allowance is about the same as Newstart, which is the equivalent of $10 000 in the first year. Log onto www.jobsearch. gov.au for more information, or contact Centrelink on 132 850.

There's no doubt that being flexible enough to consider the different options of starting up your own business, working from home or subcontracting your talents is a real plus. And many people who have gone through redundancy use part of their payout to set up their own business or consultancy. It can be a great move, but bear in mind that not everyone succeeds, and even those who do often find it takes longer than expected to generate a decent cash flow.

I'm all for setting up your own business, and I certainly wish anyone doing so all the best, but think carefully before taking on a complete career change. Don't underestimate the benefits of experience – it is vital in building up contacts and industry-specific knowledge. Indeed, before leaping into the complete unknown, you might be better off considering a change to a field with some similarity to your own. This way, you are more likely to be able to use the skills you already have, while adopting new ones. However, if you do pursue this option, I thoroughly recommend that you get in touch with one of the small business advisory services which operate in all states, providing good advice at a low cost. Take a look at Chapter 7 for more information on running a small business.

Undertake training if necessary

Rather than setting up your own business, it may be easier to invest some time retraining for a different type of job. Statistics show that redundancy is highest among low-skilled men, with one ABS report saying that unless these workers get some skills and training under their belt, they could be left behind in the job market. But ongoing training is not something that should be limited to the unskilled.

If your skills lie in an area of work that has poor long-term prospects, it is important to be open to undertaking different roles, even being prepared to retrain for them. It doesn't mean your existing skills will be wasted – far from it. Recruitment experts reckon we can expect to have several careers during our working lives, and employers are increasingly looking for breadth, as well as depth, of experience.

Aim for where the jobs are

The employment landscape is changing at an ever-accelerating pace, especially in high-tech areas where a new product or process can generate, or wipe out, whole categories of jobs seemingly before the rest of us even realise something's going on. So, one of the most important strategies for landing a job or building a career that's likely to have legs is choosing to work in a growth industry.

Those areas that have good job prospects are listed on the web site of the Department of Employment and Workplace Relations (DEWR) at www.jobsearch.gov.au, and the prospects and pay for just about every occupation imaginable are covered here.

According to DEWR, there are some clear winners in the race for jobs, and one area with good prospects is the 'services sector', which already employs over 75% of Australia's workforce. This sector includes community services, the wholesale and retail trades, public administration and defence, finance, property and business services, and recreational services.

While highly skilled occupations enjoy the best job prospects looking ahead, there are still opportunities for less skilled workers. I've already noted the growth in retailing, for example, which is expected to create tremendous demand for checkout operators and sales assistants, and high job turnover in this area means plenty of openings for job seekers. Other low-skill jobs that DEWR rates as having a good future include nannies, taxi drivers and gardeners.

Qualities that should see you re-employed

There's no doubt that jobs are not as easy to come by as they once were, and while a university degree or other tertiary education will stand you in good stead, there are certain skills and abilities that are always in demand.

Flexibility No, you don't have to be a contortionist – unless you intend to work as a yoga instructor. Flexibility is more about coping with change. Successful businesses need to be able to turn on a sixpence these days, so it's not unreasonable to expect the same of their employees. Flexibility is about being prepared to go beyond your job specifications, being willing to take on training, or even just being open to work overtime.

Computer literacy Look, no one expects you to be a computer expert, but the fact is that computers and information technology (IT) are an integral part of the way we live and many jobs are based around computers. So it makes sense to be comfortable using technology, no matter what you're doing, even if it's just mastering the basics of using email, word processing and spreadsheets. If you feel the need to upgrade your skills or education in any area, a good place to begin is in IT, and the good news is that many community colleges offer some valuable courses at very low cost.

There are a whole host of other qualities that employers value which will be, and always have been, important in the workplace. I'm talking here about things like creativity, adaptability and being able to communicate and work as part of a team. Now, I freely acknowledge that I am no recruitment expert, but over nearly two decades in business, I have been involved in just about every aspect of staff hiring, and I reckon these sorts of personal characteristics rate high on most employers' lists of 'must-haves'. One final thing that will always be welcomed by any boss is a 'can do' attitude. Sometimes this last quality can make you a better candidate than other more experienced or better qualified applicants.

Improve your job prospects

Take time to plan your next move Taking on part-time or contract work for the short term will relieve some of the financial pressure while you take time to assess your options and do some career planning or retraining. It is often tempting to leap into the first job that becomes available, but we spend a lot of time at work, so it makes sense to invest some time into getting it right.

Do some research When you're looking for a job, it pays to find out a bit about the organisation you want to work for – and a good first step is finding out who you should speak to about work. Nothing leaves a personnel manager colder than a job application addressed to 'Dear Sir or Madam'. When you contact a business, let them know who you are and why you are calling and tell them you would like to send in a resume. If you don't feel comfortable doing this, at least ask about what sort of skills and qualifications the organisation is looking for in employees – this should give you an idea of any retraining you might need to do.

Tap the hidden job market According to the ABS, only about 17% of jobs are found through newspaper or Internet advertising. That means you need to find out where the jobs are yourself. Don't be afraid to spread the word among friends, relatives and other business and social contacts that you are available for work. When you think about how many people we know, whether it's through our children or through sport and hobbies, there are literally hundreds of people out there who could help you get a job.

Have a professional resume I have seen some great resumes in my time and I have seen some real duds. A resume speaks volumes about the person writing it, and sending a lacklustre resume to a potential employer immediately cuts your chances short. Spending some time and money having your resume professionally prepared can be a good investment.

There's nothing to say that you can't send out slightly different resumes to different employers. Tailor each resume to the job description emphasising your skills or qualifications according to the description. But stick to a limit of three pages (preferably just two), and be sure to address all selection criteria and qualities outlined in the advertisement.

Try to send your resume out by email wherever email addresses are given as it really speeds things up (and it's cheaper).

Don't give up! If you are aiming to find a similar job to the one you left, allow yourself plenty of time. Statistics show that the average time taken to get work can range from eight weeks for teenagers and up to 22 weeks for the over-55s. It can take even longer if you are looking for a particularly senior or well-paid role. In the interim period, treat the hunt for work as a job in itself. Studies have shown that many people give up the job hunt early, often scaling down their efforts to about six hours a week. When you think about it, it makes sense that you'll have a better strike rate just by making job hunting a full-time project. In the meantime, consulting or contract work is a good way to keep your skills up to date as well as getting a foot in the door.

Whatever you decide, bear in mind those with a positive outlook, determination and a flexible approach seem to do best.

TIPS FOR SURVIVING REDUNDANCY

- Budget for a period of unemployment.
- Let your network of friends and business contacts know you are available.
- Don't limit your career options to a role similar to the one you just left.
- Job hunt early – it could take longer than you think.

Useful contacts	Web site/telephone number
Australian Jobsearch – Department of Employment and Workplace Relations	www.jobsearch.gov.au
Business Entry Point	www.business.gov.au
Career information service	www.myfuture.edu.au
Centrelink Employment Service	www.centrelink.gov.au Ph: 132 850
Job Network	www.jobnetwork.gov.au
New Apprenticeships Centres	www.newapprenticeships.gov.au Ph: 1800 639 629

Rates of Newstart Allowance per fortnight

Family situation	Amount per fortnight
Single, aged 21 or over, no children	$380
Single, aged 21 or over, with children	$411
Single, aged 60 or over, after nine months	$416
Partnered (each)	$342

Source: Centrelink, as at March 2003.

Newstart Allowance income test

Family situation	For full payment (per fortnight)	For part payment (per fortnight)
Single, aged 21 or over	Up to $62 of other income	Less than $627
Single, aged over 60, after nine months, or on MAA	Up to $62 of other income	Less than $680
Single, aged over 18, with dependent children	Up to $62 of other income	Less than $672
Partnered, aged over 18 with children, or aged over 21, each	Up to $62 of other income	Less than $574

Source: Centrelink, as at March 2003.

Newstart Allowance assets test

Family situation	Asset limit for full allowance
Homeowners	
Single	up to $145 250
Partnered (combined)	up to $206 500
Non-homeowners	
Single	up to $249 750
Partnered (combined)	up to $311 000

Source: Centrelink, as at March 2003.

7

Small business, big trouble

Many people see running a small business as something of a gamble. You could hit the jackpot and make a fortune; you might walk away having broken even; or you could lose the lot. But going into business for yourself is less risky than most people think. Sure, most of us have come across horror figures saying that something like 60% of businesses fail in the first five years. And when you come across these sorts of claims it's easy to believe that success in small business is either very rare, or hard to achieve. But, according to a report by the Productivity Commission,* many small businesses are around for a surprisingly long time, with two-thirds still operating after five years and almost half still going a decade after they started. Even after 15 years, it seems that around one-third of businesses will have survived.

---

* I. Bickerdyke, R. Lattimore & A. Madge, 'Business Failure and Change: An Australian Perspective', Productivity Commission, December 2000. See www.pc.gov.au/research/staffres/bfacaap/index.html/

And just because a business disappears, it doesn't automatically mean it has failed. Some businesses are sold, some change names, and in other cases the owner may just decide to retire. In fact, the Productivity Commission found that less than 1% of small businesses close because of insolvency or bankruptcy (technically speaking, if the business is run through a company, it goes into 'liquidation', whereas if it is run by a sole trader it goes into 'bankruptcy').

While around 7% of small businesses leave the scene each year, up to double this number enter the market annually. And let's be thankful they do. Small businesses are a key part of our economy, providing just under half of all jobs.

Speak to a successful small business operator and they will generally tell you that the tough times and hard work (of which there is usually plenty) have all been worthwhile. And while not every business will grow into a BHP or a Woolworths, a thriving business can provide you with a decent income and, hopefully, an enjoyable lifestyle as well as an enormous sense of achievement.

I reckon going into business can be a great idea, but I know from my own experience in co-founding ipac securities what a tremendous financial challenge it can be. And while many small ventures thrive, there are lots that struggle along or never quite realise their full potential. Yet despite what the self-help spivs might try to tell you, there is no proven formula for success in business. However, there are definitely problems that are common to just about all businesses – old or new, large or small, and if you can navigate your way around these, you'll be much further down the road to business success.

Hopefully you won't recognise all of the warning signs in your own business, but even if just one of them sounds familiar, it could be time for action as these indicators tend to be a sign, if not of failure, then certainly of lost profits.

COMMON SMALL BUSINESS PROBLEMS (AND HOW TO FIX THEM)

'I can't manage the business – the business manages me!'

There are plenty of minefields for the owners of a small business but the biggest by far is the lack of management experience. Many people go into business believing that because they are good at what they do, they will be good at running a business that does the same thing. It's the 'I'm a good plumber so I'll be good at running a plumbing business' line of thinking. This is not always the case, because operating a small business adds a whole new dimension – looking after the business itself. This means keeping books, withholding and paying a variety of taxes, meeting various statutory obligations, looking after customers and staff, collecting debts, paying creditors, managing cash flow and so on. In fact, research suggests that the vast majority of those businesses that do fail are victims of poor management, with poor sales, bad location or economic downturn all coming a distant second.

Let me put it this way. In small business things can sometimes be run in a bit of an off-the-cuff way. That's fine for lots of ventures when they're just starting up and things are small. But when the business starts to grow, the owners often face challenges that they are too busy, too unprepared or too inexperienced to deal with. Everyone wants their business to thrive, but sadly many people just can't control the horse once it starts to gallop away.

For those going into business for the first time, there will be a steep learning curve with many 'firsts' encountered along the way – first time collecting debts, first time hiring staff, and so on. Unless you feel you can allow for the time involved in getting to the top of that learning curve, I would thoroughly recommend some sort of management training. All you need is a grounding in the basics, so it does not have to be anything more than a simple business skills course. And it needn't cost you an arm and a leg. A number of government departments (listed at the end of this chapter) provide free or low-cost management training.

'I don't have a business plan!'

Planning plays an important role in many aspects of our lives. We draw up plans for how our homes will be built, we plan for the number of children we have (things sometimes go awry in this area, but it's the thought that counts), and we even plan our holidays. But it never ceases to amaze me how many people go into business, sometimes at great personal expense, without a plan at all.

So, what is a business plan? Well, it is a written statement of what your business involves, where it is heading and how it will get there. It gives you something to measure the performance of the business by, so that one, two or three years down the track you can have another look at whether or not you are getting what you want from the venture.

It's also something that lenders will want to see if you apply for finance, so it's a good idea to always have a reasonably up-to-date business plan on hand.

What a business plan should show A business plan can be as broad or as detailed as you want to make it, but the two things it must have are a description of your business and some key financial details.

1. A description of your business

This part of the business plan will be more important if you are writing it to attract investors or get finance, as you will need to be able to convince some potentially sceptical readers that your business is a good one. This section should include:

- a description of what your business does – your product or service, and how the business will be run
- the outlook of the industry in which you work (for example, tourism, publishing, retailing and so on)

- a description of your market (who your customers are)
- who your competitors are
- who your suppliers are
- your marketing strategy – how you will get new business and beat the competition, and
- a description of your experience in this industry – in other words, why you think you will succeed.

2. Financial details

This is really the nuts and bolts part of your plan which will tell you and anyone else reading it whether or not you are going to turn a profit. No matter who will be reading it, you need to be as realistic in your calculations and estimates as possible. After all, the last thing you want is the expense and heartbreak of running a business that never really stood a chance of making a profit.

When it comes to financial details, there are umpteen variations on what you could include, but there are two pieces of information that are absolutely critical:

- *A profit and loss forecast.* You'll need to estimate your sales and expenses on a month-by-month basis to determine whether or not you are likely to bring in a profit. Remember to allow for seasonal variations that may affect the business. For example, retail businesses often rate Christmas as their busiest period, while others, like accounting firms, find it is a quiet time. New business ventures will need to include an estimate of start-up costs.
- *A cash flow forecast.* This is probably more important than the profit and loss forecast. You see, even though you may be making a profit on paper, if you don't have sufficient cash coming in each month to pay for the following month's stock purchases and wages, your business will soon be in real trouble. (More on this later.)

Writing a business plan might seem a bit daunting but it is reasonably straightforward. The key is to be realistic when it comes to making projections and forecasts and this is where your experience in the industry or in running a business to date will help. If estimates and figures are not your strong suit, get an accountant to give you some help (anyone who is serious about being in business needs a decent accountant anyway).

'I can't control my cash flow!'

The best way to approach the whole cash flow concept is to think of cash as the lifeblood of your business. Yes, sales are important, but cash is critical. Without adequate cash a whole series of unpleasant events begin to unfold. First, you find yourself unable to pay creditors on time, so they start putting the squeeze on you. Then, you begin relying on high-interest finance like overdrafts or credit cards to pay creditors, and with little money to reinvest back into the business to help it grow, a thriving venture can quickly start to freefall.

There are two equally important sides to cash management: 'debt management' – that's the cash coming in from your debtors (people who owe you money); and 'credit management' – involving how you time your payments to creditors (the people you owe money to). Both are critical, and they are certainly important enough to be looked at separately.

Debt management – turn sales into cash In small business, the person at the helm is often a terrific salesperson, but mention debt collection to them and they hastily change the subject. But it's important to realise that every sale has two parts: making the sale *and* collecting the revenue. When businesses are facing financial difficulties, it's a common mistake to think that the way out is by increasing sales. But unless the revenue is actually coming into your bank account, it's a strategy that can do more harm than good.

That's because sales have associated costs – commission to sales people, the cost of stock, shipping and freight, and so on. And unless the sales are being converted into cash, the business can start to face serious cash shortages even though revenues are apparently healthy. So, collecting the money is just as important as making the sale in the first place, and here are some ways to do it.

1. Invoice small – invoice often

Debtors who drag their feet are not always the cause of cash flow problems. In small business, it's easy for the owner to get caught up in the daily running of the venture, simply forgetting to bill clients and only taking action when the cash dries up. At that point, they go into crisis mode, frantically sending out huge bills to customers who then become irate at being hit with one enormous invoice, and who themselves may not have the funds to pay one hefty bill.

Preparing and sending out invoices on a regular basis will certainly take up some of your time, but it's a critical part of taking care of your cash. The policy of billing small amounts often, works because your debtors find it easier to pay small, regular bills than to be slugged with one large one out of the blue. And it evens out your cash flow as well as theirs.

2. Collect the cash

Having sent out an invoice, the next step is to collect the cash. No one, with the possible exception of professional repo men, likes chasing up debts, but consider this. What starts off as a healthy bank balance can quickly dwindle to a costly overdraft if your debtors are paying you on 60-day terms and you are paying your creditors in 30 days. From here it can be a downward spiral where creditors cut off supplies because of *your* late payments. You then have less cash to pay staff, less to reinvest in the business and, ultimately, less to live on yourself.

If your debtors are dragging the chain, it's time to take a two-pronged approach. First, start actively collecting your outstanding debtors. This doesn't mean employing the local hoods to 'rough up' a few customers, it simply means giving debtors gentle reminders of their outstanding balances. Forget the fluoro stickers depicting a knot tied around a finger – sometimes they just don't cut the mustard. Instead, try issuing slow payers with a statement a week or two after they've been billed and make a follow-up telephone call a week later. Don't settle for a 'cheque's in the mail' response. Instead, suggest a time when it's convenient for you or a courier to pick up the cheque. Only offer a payment instalment plan as a last resort, as you could find yourself wasting even more time chasing up small instalments instead of the total amount you're owed.

The second, more drastic, approach is to stop offering credit terms to debtors who repeatedly drag their feet. Instead, offer 'cash on delivery' or ask for cash upfront until their account is reduced to balances aged 30 days or less. Sometimes you need to make it clear that you cannot continue to supply goods or a service until payment is made and, ultimately, you need to think about whether you want this customer or not.

Understandably, small business owners are often concerned that drastic measures will see them lose customers. But when you think about it, you are only applying the principles that *your* creditors have applied to you. The fact is, some customers are just more trouble than they're worth, and if they are consistently bad payers, don't be afraid to ditch them.

3. Set the ground rules early

Making the terms of payment clear up-front is one way of avoiding debtor problems. It is always exciting to get a new customer and you may feel tempted to offer overly generous discounts and credit terms just to get their business in the first place, but by doing this you are establishing a pattern for the future that may be hard to live with.

Small early payment discounts are often effective to encourage prompt payment from debtors. Depending on the nature of your business, you can make it easier for your debtors to pay by offering EFTPOS or payment by credit cards. You will pay a merchant fee for this (up to about 3% of each transaction), but most small businesses report that it makes for quicker payment.

If you are experiencing a cash crunch, there are a couple of steps you can take to free up some funds.

- Consider leasing equipment rather than buying it, especially if you only need it for short-term use.
- Keep a careful eye on your stock levels and only buy in bulk when you are sure the entire quantity can be used up.
- Be ruthless about any slow-moving stock lines by offering them at marked-down prices.
- A lot of your office equipment probably doesn't need to be state of the art. Keep an eye out for newspaper advertisements for liquidators' auctions of office equipment and furniture. You will be able to pick up items at a fraction of their normal retail price.

Credit management – take care of your creditors As anyone who has fallen behind in their credit card payments can tell you, the downside of credit is that small amounts can build up to big ones in seemingly no time at all. The same applies in business. But the difference here is that you need supplies from your creditors to make your business work. You may have invested a great deal of time sourcing the right supplies and negotiating a good price, so it makes sense to stay on good terms with a creditor while at the same time making full use of the credit terms you are offered.

If you're offered an early payment discount it can be well worth taking advantage of it, but only if the cash is available. There is not much to be gained from using an overdraft charging 7% interest to get an early payment discount of, say, 5%.

Small businesses need to be wary that creditors sometimes take far more serious action to recover an unpaid bill than the owner may have expected. If your business is unincorporated (run as a sole trader or in a partnership), you only need to owe $2000 to a creditor for them to take action to have you made bankrupt. And it is not uncommon for an otherwise solvent business to be sent to the wall this way – taking the hapless owner completely by surprise.

If you are having problems paying your creditors, I strongly recommend that you take a look at Chapter 4, as many of the principles that apply to individuals also apply to business.

Don't forget the taxman's take It's the oldest pitfall around – to see the end of the day balances as far larger than they really are, forgetting to allow for tax. These days, small businesses have to plan for, withhold and pay a variety of taxes and imposts ranging from the Goods and Services Tax (GST) to compulsory superannuation for employees. And just as a creditor can get quite irate if you don't cough up the cash, you can get into some very hot water if you don't set sufficient funds aside to meet your tax obligations.

'I have to do it all myself!'

Successful business people know their business like the back of their hand, but they don't try to *do* it all themselves. Just attempting to do everything yourself is likely to age you quick smart, especially once the business starts to expand. But it doesn't just rest with some extra grey hairs. You see, one of the best things you can do in small business is to develop the venture to the point where it could survive without you. If it can't, you may just be buying yourself a job. The business may be your pride and joy today, but the time may come when you want out, and it is very hard to sell a business whose success depends heavily on the owner being around.

The first step in building a business that doesn't rely entirely on you is to take on, and entrust work to, your employees. If you cannot hand over increasing amounts of work to your staff, even modest growth in your enterprise will swamp you. If you are in a service business, you also need to make it clear to clients and customers that while you are always there to help them, you will be handing over at least some of the work to a staff member.

As the owner of the business, make it your aim to gradually phase yourself out of the day-to-day operations, aiming for more of an overview role where you are working *on* developing the business rather than *in* the nuts and bolts of the business.

Let me stress again that many small businesses thrive, and those that struggle are generally the minority. That is not to say that it's all beer and skittles. Running your own business can involve long hours and big responsibility. But one of the biggest mistakes you can make is waiting until a small problem becomes a big one. If you see trouble brewing, it is important to take action early while the problem is still manageable.

FINANCING FOR SMALL BUSINESS

Funding is critical for any small business, yet because of their size and often unproven track record, it can be a challenge to get finance. Additional funds can come from two sources: third party debt, provided by the likes of banks or finance companies; or an additional shot of equity, either from the existing proprietor or new ones. There are pros and cons with both options, and anyone running a business should run them past their accountant before making a decision.

Debt financing

In Australia the bulk of business financing comes from the banks. Irrespective of the debt that you apply for – be it an overdraft or a secured loan – the lender will look at three things:

- why you need the money (this should be business-related)
- the business's ability to service the debt – in other words, how easily you can repay both the interest and principal, and
- the security you can offer the lender – in other words, whether there are any assets that the lender can take possession of if you can't repay.

It is this last requirement – security – which is often the sticking point for many small ventures. I said at the start of this chapter that most small businesses aren't as risky as we tend to think, but the first few years are still the danger period. Remember that Productivity Commission report (page 132) which said around two-thirds of small enterprises will still be going after five years? Well, that still leaves a failure rate of around 30% in the early years – and those are not good odds for the banks that are lending money to you.

So, lenders are often reluctant to provide loans that are secured by the assets of the business until it can show stable earnings, a steady gross margin on its sales, good quality debtors and steady stock turnover. These all take time to establish, and from the bank's point of view, there is no certainty that the business assets that provide security today will still be there tomorrow. That's why the owner's family home is the most commonly used form of security for small business loans.

Of course, if the business is using the funds to buy a major asset like, say, a truck, the asset itself may be sufficient security. However, overdrafts are particularly worrisome for bank managers, as theoretically there is nothing to stop you drawing down the lot and shooting through to Rio.

Readers regularly write in to *Money Magazine* asking about where they can get a loan to start their own business. Unfortunately, because of the risks involved, if you don't have a residential property that you can put forward as security, it is difficult to get a business loan irrespective of whether you use a bank, building society or finance company. In this case, your best option may be equity funding – more on this later.

Bearing in mind that you may be asked to put up the family home as security when you apply for bank finance, your lender will want to see:

- a copy of your business plan
- the documents of incorporation if the business is run through a company, or the registration of your business name if you operate as a sole trader, and
- around three years' worth of financial statements.

Clearly, if the business plan and financial statements are prepared by a qualified accountant they will carry a lot more force than something that has been knocked up on the back of a beer coaster. And thanks largely to the GST, the days when one set of books was drawn up for the bank and another set was presented to the taxman are just about over. As part of its audit process, the Tax Office has the right to look at the bank's records to see why money was lent to a business which may have been consistently reporting tax losses. So the accounts you present to a lender should bear more than a passing resemblance to the figures you have reported to the taxman.

It's a good idea to make your existing lender your first port of call. The bank or credit union you have a home mortgage or other personal borrowings with will have a proven track record of your repayment ability as well as existing security. But be careful about the assets you put up as security on business loans. If the business goes belly up, it is an easy way to lose everything.

Non-conforming lenders Non-conforming lenders are an alternative to the more mainstream lenders, providing finance to small businesses and the self-employed who may not meet standard lending requirements. They charge higher interest rates than the banks, reflecting the greater risk involved, and they too generally want residential property to be used as security. For more information on these lenders, take a look at Chapter 5.

Equity funding

For businesses unable (or unwilling) to put up security, financing can be hard to come by, which goes a long way towards explaining why credit card debt can be as much a problem for small ventures as it is for consumers. But a cheaper alternative is 'equity' funding. This involves introducing additional shareholders or partners who put in extra capital (called equity) and who get a share of the profits in return.

The beauty of equity funding is that it's far cheaper than debt. If the business fails to turn a profit, your new partner or shareholder generally doesn't get a return. On the other hand, a bank loan calls for interest to be repaid regardless of whether or not the business made a cent.

Many people starting or expanding a business venture turn to family and friends for equity funding, but this limits the extent of your capital raising and it could pay to look further afield.

Enter 'business angels'. These are people who invest their money and their skills in a small enterprise. As well as being a potentially low-cost source of funds, business angels let you tap into an additional source of knowledge and experience. On the downside, though, there is a lot that could go wrong, so it pays for the investor and the existing owner of the business to thoroughly scrutinise what's being offered, as well as the people involved.

There are a number of organisations that can help put you in touch with a business angel, but a good starting point is the

Australian Venture Capital Association. Their web address is www.avcal.com.au or they can be contacted on 02 9251 3888.

There's no promotion like self-promotion

Self-promotion doesn't come naturally to many of us, but remember circus master P. T. Barnum's favourite expression: 'Without promotion something terrible happens. Nothing.'

WHERE TO GET HELP

The following small business advisory services provide good, low-cost support services for business operators. In addition to running cheap or free seminars, workshops and providing advice, they also publish numerous pamphlets and booklets on business basics. It may involve some of your time to access and use them, but it usually doesn't cost much at all and I recommend you take advantage of these services.

State	Service	Contact number
ACT	Canberra Business Advisory Service	02 6260 5000
New South Wales	Sydney Business Enterprise Centre	02 9282 6977
Northern Territory	Northern Territory Business Centre	08 8924 4280
Queensland	Department of State Development	07 3224 8568
South Australia	Centre for Innovation, Business and Manufacturing	08 8233 4600
Tasmania	Department of Economic Development	03 6233 5712
Victoria	Business Access	03 9651 9888
Western Australia	WA Small Business & Enterprise Association	08 9322 2854

8

Suddenly single – separation and divorce

There is no doubt that going through separation and divorce is one of the toughest times in anyone's life. It's tough emotionally, it can be hard socially and, there is no doubt, it can be a real battle financially. But with Australian Bureau of Statistics (ABS) figures projecting a divorce rate of around 32% of all marriages, it's a reality of modern life.

But while our marriage break-up rate of one in three may sound pretty high, it's still relatively low compared to that of Belarus, where 68% of marriages fail, or even Sweden, where the figure is 64%. And in the US, where things tend to be bigger if not better, divorce has become a 'thriving' industry, supporting a range of clubs, publications and web sites like 'DivorceMag.com – for generation "ex"', featuring the must-read column, 'Ask Ivana Trump'. Even the stodgy British legal fraternity has jumped on the bandwagon, with one up-market law firm making headlines when it attempted to drum up business for its family law division by taking out a series of magazine ads headed 'Ditch the Bitch'.

Fortunately, in Australia divorce is still regarded as something not to be taken lightly, and rightly so. Apart from the emotional upheaval it involves, it can cause serious financial setbacks, often because the same amount of money is coming in, but more is going out on the extra costs associated with legal fees (which under family law are paid for by both parties), establishing a second home and paying off joint debts (like credit cards), which may become the sole responsibility of one former spouse.

The 'ex' files

Over a lifespan of 77 years, the 'average man' would spend 42 years as a bachelor, 28 years married, 5 years divorced and 2 years as a widower.

For a woman, with a lifespan of 82 years, the equivalent figures are 40 years as a spinster, 29 years married, 7 years divorced, and 6 years widowed.

Source: ABS Marriages and Divorces, Australia 2000.

HOW THE FAMILY COURT WORKS

If you and your spouse decide to part ways you'll need to apply to the Family Court for a divorce, also known as 'dissolution of marriage'. While this may mark the legal end of your marriage, it doesn't settle issues about how your property is to be shared or how the children are to be looked after. These have to be dealt with in separate applications to the court, and a divorce may not be granted at all if there are unresolved matters relating to the children.

People are sometimes surprised to learn that the Family Law Act does not consider the causes of the marriage breakdown. It's what's known as a 'no-fault' system, where the only requirement is that the marriage is broken beyond repair. I mention this because it means the court doesn't usually consider the actions of either spouse when determining settlements.

It is also worth noting that the Family Court can hear disputes about arrangements for children following the breakdown of any relationship, but where your finances are concerned, the Family Court can only make decisions regarding married couples. Financial disputes between de facto couples are heard in the state or territory courts (the Family Court being part of the Commonwealth system).

PROPERTY – TO HAVE AND TO HOLD ONTO

One of the hurdles facing separating couples is dividing their property. You can physically divvy up the assets between yourselves, or alternatively you can sell the lot and split the proceeds. Whichever strategy you opt for, this is one area where it pays to see an accredited family law specialist (the Law Society in your state can point you in the right direction).

When it comes to agreements involving a transfer of assets between spouses, you need either an agreement which includes an independent certificate of advice from your solicitor or an order of the court approving the settlement. Without one of these you could end up being slugged with a stamp duty or capital gains tax bill that could otherwise have been avoided when you transfer your assets from one spouse to another. The tax rules here are complex (as usual), and couples who take the do-it-yourself route may find they end up paying more to the taxman than they would have to a solicitor.

Having the court approve the financial settlement also marks a defining point where each spouse usually no longer has a right to their ex's property. You generally need to have been apart for a year before applying for a divorce, but court proceedings for property orders can begin as soon as you have separated. Some couples wait for years before finalising their property settlement, only to find the delay can cost them dearly. That's because the Family Court looks at the assets held by both parties at the time of the hearing, *not* the time of the separation. People often build up assets in the intervening period, and even if it's through an inheritance or a windfall (like a big win on the pokies), it can all be up for grabs in the final settlement.

In one case I read about, a divorcing couple had few assets to speak of at the time of their separation, but 18 months down the track, the ex-husband won a handy $5 million in a lottery. When the case came in front of the Family Court, the judge held that even though the wife had not contributed to the cost of the winning lottery ticket, she had certainly contributed to raising the family, and so she was entitled to a share of the winnings. Clearly, though, this is an extreme case and, sadly, few of us will ever have the 'problem' of dividing up, say, a big lotto win.

Family law experts agree that the best approach in terms of saving money, time and stress is to have your facts ready *before* you go to see a solicitor. Get together the paperwork for all your assets, including information on when they were purchased as well as their approximate values. Don't forget to include super statements and the value of any life insurance policies. You also need a list of all your personal liabilities including mortgages and personal loans. From here your solicitor (and I stress the need to go to a family law specialist) can put together a range of options that you can realistically and legally expect in a settlement (the court won't approve a settlement that doesn't appear fair to both parties).

Yes, you will pay legal fees for this, but if you can keep the lines of communication open, you stand a better chance of benefiting from the assets you worked so hard for in the first place. It also lets you make a fresh start in life sooner, rather than after years of costly court wrangling.

One way to save money is through 'mediation'. You still need to go to a solicitor first to find out what you are legally entitled to, but then you sit with a mediator, who acts as an independent third party, to work through who gets what. If the discussion starts to get a bit heated, the mediator steps in to keep the negotiations on track.

Mediation is considerably cheaper than legal fees, and research has shown that couples are more likely to stick with an agreement that they come to themselves. Note, though, the Family Court also offers the option of mediation at every stage of the settlement process and fortunately only a very small percentage of divorcing couples – usually around 5% of cases – get to final hearing stage.

An agreement made with a mediator is not legally binding, so you'll still have to get your solicitor to formalise the agreement in writing. Mediation works best where the property arrangements are reasonably straightforward. If you have very complex financial arrangements where assets are held in the name of, say, companies or trusts, it may be better to stick with a solicitor, some of whom are also trained in mediation.

WHICH WAY THE ASSETS WILL GO

Couples who cannot agree on a property settlement may need to start proceedings in the Family Court, but there are several reasons why I urge you not to let things get to this stage. First, it can be costly and drawn out. On the *Money* show we met one divorcee who had spent seven years and over $40 000 finalising a settlement. Secondly, when it comes to property disputes, the current system is discretionary, meaning there are no hard and fast rules about who gets what, and you may not finish up in the position you'd hoped for. The decision, made by a judge, takes into account what you have, what you owe, the contributions made to the marriage by each partner (homemakers usually being given as much credit as breadwinners), your future requirements and your financial resources, including your ability to earn an income.

A 2001 study* of property settlements by the Australian Institute of Family Studies (AIFS) found that, on average, the wife is awarded just over half the value of the property (which usually consists of the house, its contents, a car and super). But as the average value of the net assets to be split (excluding super) was $124 000, it is by no means a get-rich-quick option.

The same study went on to say that while it is impossible to predict what the final cut will be, the lion's share of a couple's basic assets – essentially the family home – has consistently been allocated to the parent with whom the children live, and in almost every case this is their mother. Just over half of all divorces involve children and an amazing 94% of children up to age four live with their mother. This percentage falls as the children get older, but even among teenagers, around 80% live with their mum. Take note, though, that the court won't hesitate to make orders for the home to be sold if that's what it takes to make a fair distribution of the assets.

SUPERANNUATION

Nowadays, super makes up a far larger proportion of our wealth (about a quarter of our net assets), than it has in the past. That's great news from a retirement perspective, but for separating couples it has become a real sticking point. That's because super entitlements are not 'vested' (that is, not yet available to the contributor – usually because they haven't reached retirement age) and are not 'property' in the way that, say, a house or a car is. For many years, this left the Family Court unable to make direct orders

---

* G. Sheehan & J. Hughes, 'Division of Matrimonial Property in Australia', Australian Institute of Family Studies, Research Paper no. 25, March 2001.

over super. In addition, the Superannuation Act didn't allow the transfer of super between spouses on separation (or for any other reason) and, to make matters worse, the courts had no clear power to make orders against super fund trustees. The picture was made even bleaker by the fact that the wife, often having exchanged a career for raising a family, had little, if any, super in her own name – around $5500 on average, compared to just over $22 000 for men.

The result was no consistent treatment of super. In some cases it was simply ignored, which left the ex-wife out of pocket. In other instances, the entire case was adjourned until the contributing spouse approached retirement age – which left couples without a clean break. In other cases again, the value of the super was offset against the family home, which left the ex-husband with an asset that he couldn't touch for many years.

This situation has been turned around by changes to Family Law, which only came into effect in December 2002. Like all new legislation, there may be some finetuning done along the way but, as it stands, it is not essential for each spouse to have contributed to the super to get a share of the loot. The non-contributing spouse has access to their former partner's superannuation accounts and, under the new legislation, can even gain access without their consent.

The way the super nest egg is valued depends on the type of fund. With 'accumulation' funds, which are by far the most popular, the super's value is simply the amount that has been building up from contributions and investment earnings in the account. So it's simply a matter of carving up what's already there.

The picture is not so clear-cut with 'defined benefit' funds. With these funds, your final payout is 'defined' by a set formula. For example, you may get four times your salary if you retire at 55, five times at age 60 and so on. The new super legislation includes a method for valuing your interest in these schemes, or alternatively the court can put a hold on any withdrawals from the fund, so that no one can touch the money without court approval.

Once the super has been valued, it is up to the couple (or the court) to work out how it should be split, using either a percentage basis, a dollar amount or even swapping the lot for another asset. If the super is to be split, and if the type of fund allows it, the non-member spouse has several options. You can choose to set up an account in your ex's fund, although some funds (for example, those open only to employees) may not let you do this. If that's the case, the only option is to roll the money over to another fund. You can roll the money over to a fund of your choice, or, under some circumstances, you may be able to cash the money out of super altogether.

It's also possible to delay a final agreement on how the nest egg will be shared until the member spouse meets a condition of release for the funds; for example, retiring at 55, or reaching the pension age.

The seven-year itch?

Forget about getting itchy feet after seven years. According to the ABS, 17% of divorces happen within the first five years of marriage, while a further 26% of couples go their separate ways within the next five years.

Source: ABS Cat. 3310.0 2001.

SPOUSAL MAINTENANCE

We've all heard stories about the multi-million dollar payouts made by the rich and famous to their exes, but for ordinary families, the outlook is not so good. Under Australian family law there is no hard and fast law that says you have to pay spousal mainte-nance (as distinct from child support). An ex-spouse may only be called on to give financial support to a former partner where they are in a 'reasonable position' to do so and where their ex 'cannot adequately support themselves'. It's all very stern stuff, but the fact is that spousal maintenance is uncommon in Australia and at best it is only intended as a temporary measure.

To give you an indication of what you can (or more likely, cannot) expect, one survey found that maintenance is awarded in less than 7% of divorces, and even then it usually only amounts to $130 a week, lasting for around two years (source: AIFS).

Again, there are no hard and fast rules about how much maintenance you *may* get (or be asked to pay), but the court will look at each partner's age, health, income, property and financial resources, their ability to earn their own income and any child care obligations.

GOVERNMENT SUPPORT

When you find yourself suddenly single through separation, divorce, or even the death of a spouse, you may be eligible for one or more of the government allowances paid through Centrelink.

Family Tax Benefit and Parenting Payment

Single parents may be eligible for the Family Tax Benefit and Parenting Payment. These payments are covered in Chapter 3.

Widow Allowance

This is actually something of a misnomer as it is also available to women who have become divorced or separated since turning 40. To be eligible, you will need to be aged 50 or over, single and have no recent work experience. Widow Allowance for 2002/03 starts at around $380 per fortnight, but this amount is adjusted periodically in line with the cost of living.

The payments are subject to both an income test (you can earn up to $62 each fortnight before the allowance is reduced at the rate of 50 cents in the dollar), and an assets test (homeowners have a limit of $145 250, while the limit for non-homeowners is $249 750).

Other payments or concessions you may be entitled to include rental assistance and a pharmaceutical allowance.

CHILD SUPPORT

It's probably stating the obvious to say that children are a wonderful but expensive addition to our lives and, as any single parent knows, this certainly doesn't change when parents separate. It has always been the case that the parent with whom the children are living is entitled to receive child maintenance, but in years gone by it was not uncommon, following a divorce, for financial support to gradually slow to a trickle and ultimately dry up altogether. Enforcing child maintenance payments through the courts was expensive and time consuming, so many parents simply didn't bother. It was a situation that saw many families, especially single mums, doing it tough.

To improve the situation the Child Support Scheme, run through the Child Support Agency (CSA), was introduced in the late 1980s. The scheme took effect in October 1989, so it only applies if either you separated or your children were born after this date (in other instances, the Family Court determines how much child support is paid and by whom). The scheme has opened up a number of options for parents, ranging from agreeing on the amount of child support and making payments privately, right through to asking the CSA to calculate and collect the child support payments.

To reach a child support figure, the CSA uses a formula that takes into account each parent's income, the number of children involved, the living expenses of each parent and the living arrangements of the children. Broadly speaking, the paying parent (the one with whom the children do not live) pays child support as a percentage of their income, starting out at 18% of their income for one child, 27% if there are two children, 32% for three children, and so on. For example, let's say that a separated couple have two children, both of whom live with their mother. Dad earns $35 000 per annum, while mum earns $10 000 in a part-time job. Their father's child support obligation will be calculated at about $6100 annually or $120 weekly. You don't have to worry about doing these calculations yourself – there is a calculator on the CSA web site (located at www.csa.gov.au) where you can get a rough idea of the child support that CSA would set down, or they can be contacted by phoning 131 272.

Be aware, though, that the final payment figure can be adjusted to include things like any special needs your children may have. The payment is also recalculated each year to take into account inflation and any changes in either parent's income.

The CSA is part of the Tax Office, so if payments fall behind, the taxman has the power to deduct child support directly from the paying parent's income, intercept a tax refund, or withhold part of any Centrelink payments.

REBUILDING

Once the smoke from the break-up has cleared, divorcees and, in particular, single parents, need to make some solid financial plans. In my two decades in the investment industry, the call for help has most frequently come from single mothers and there is no doubt that single parents face additional financial challenges rebuilding their lives while they're raising children. The strategies below apply to everyone who finds themselves suddenly single, but parents with children should also take a look at Chapter 3.

A report* commissioned in 2002 by the Financial Planning Association showed that two-parent families are successfully

---

* S. Kelly & M. Toohey, 'Who are Australia's best savers?', National Centre for Social and Economic Modelling, University of Canberra, November 2002.

investing in their homes, super and other investments, but single parents may be in danger of getting left behind. The report compared the wealth accumulated by a variety of households, and of all the groups researched, lone parents fared the worst.

That's not to say the picture is entirely grim. Single parents had a good proportion of their wealth invested in the family home, which is definitely an important foundation of wealth. And once the children are older and more independent, single parents are able to focus on growing their wealth at a similar rate to everyone else.

But the study confirms that it's tough for single parents to get some savings and investments together in the early years (25 to 34). And this is what puts them on the back foot in the long run.

For people who find themselves suddenly single, there is no shortcut to wealth. It can be a slow process – but the beauty of it is that it is achievable. The first step is to start managing your money. And by that I do mean *managing* as opposed to spending. For women who may have been out of the workforce for some time, it may also be important to start investing in your own ability to earn a good income. And, finally, you need to be careful that you protect what you have. But first, let's look at the most pressing issue – how to manage your money.

MANAGE YOUR MONEY

Regardless of how much or how little you earn, there are two essential things you need to know about – budgeting and saving.

Budgeting

When people emerge from a divorce, the household budget can become badly stretched and it's often the case that savings start to disappear. But a realistic, well-thought-out budget can be a good foundation from which to tackle the financial pressures of going solo. Don't be tempted to put off budgeting and saving until your financial situation improves. It makes sense to start right away and many people find that the simple process of budgeting is what actually turns things around.

There's no getting around the fact that budgeting sets very few people's hearts racing. Part of the problem is that a budget shows us just how much money slips through our fingers – often with very little to show for it. So that's why it is so important for people moving from a double income to a single income to have one. One of the ground rules of money management is that you can't save money if you can't keep track of it and a budget will tell you where you can rein in your spending.

It is no secret that businesses (the successful ones, anyway), operate with a budget, and with good reason. Budgets keep a business on target financially and prevent money being wasted. These are goals that are worth applying to your own budget so, if it helps, start treating yourself as a 'business'. If that all sounds a bit grandiose for someone on a single income, bear in mind that the average adult, full-time wage of just over $46 000 per year works out at more than $2 million over the course of a working life. That's real money. Yet, there are too many Australians who, after a lifetime of work, end up with not very much to show for it. Having a budget is the first step to making sure this doesn't happen to you.

Impulse buying is a killer. It will break your budget and beef up your credit card bill. If impulse buying is your weak spot, try this technique next time you are tempted. Work out how many hours you would have to work to pay for the item using your *after tax* wage or salary. For example, if you earn $12 per hour after-tax, it will take you five hours to pay for a $60 pair of shoes, or ten hours to pay for a $120 jumper. When you look at things in this light, it can make those impulse buys, especially sale items, considerably less attractive.

To make things a bit easier, I have included a Budget Planner at the end of this book. It is simple to use and taking the time to fill one out could make a real difference in getting back on your feet financially.

However, if you really struggle to make a budget work, an easy solution is to 'pay yourself first'. This strategy involves setting aside a fixed percentage of your income *first*, and spending whatever is left just as you please. The tough part is working out how much of your income you can save. Aim to put away, say, 5% of your weekly income, then have that amount transferred to an appropriate savings vehicle *before* it reaches your pocket, where realistically it's as good as spent. Then the remaining 95% is yours to spend in any way you like.

The next step is to regard these savings as your future nest egg.

Saving

Single mothers make up the vast majority of lone parents, so women more so than men need to have a lifetime plan for their financial security, and it all starts with saving. I realise that for many divorcees and single parents it can be tough enough just making ends meet. But the earlier you start saving, the less you need to save to achieve a particular long-term goal. This is because the power of compounding returns (earning interest on your interest) starts to do the hard work for you.

Let's say, for example, that a single mum, Nicky, decides to put away $15 each week into an investment giving a return of 5%. If she starts at age 25, by the time she is 55 she will have accumulated around $50 000 – more than half of which is interest. If she waits until the children are older, say, when she is 40, Nicky may be in a better position to save, but to accumulate the same nest egg she will have to put away almost $50 on a weekly basis. Clearly, it's a lot less painful and far more achievable to save $15 each week rather than $50.

The secret to savings success is to make it easy, and one method I know called 'Save little, save often' is so easy it's definitely worth a try. When you come home from work or the shops, go straight to the piggy bank or moneybox and put the loose change from your pocket or your purse into it. When the moneybox is full, bank it into your savings account. When that builds up to say, $100, or even $50, take it out and, as a matter of priority, put it towards your mortgage or into another investment, be it shares or a managed fund. Just don't dip into it while it's at home.

Look for savings accounts or term deposits where interest is calculated and paid monthly or quarterly rather than annually. The more frequently interest is accrued, the higher the 'effective' rate of interest.

An account paying 4% interest calculated monthly, for example, will have an effective rate of 4.07% pa, compared to an effective rate of 4.04% pa where the calculation is made semi-annually.

In addition to the very simple technique of 'paying yourself first' or saving your change, there are dozens of ways where $10 or $20 can be put away each week. You might be amazed (or appalled), for instance, at how much you spend on seemingly little things like takeaway food, magazines, shoes, clothing, tobacco or alcohol. Cut back on these items and you can save yourself hundreds of dollars. Invest the money in quality mainstream invest-ments, and you would be amazed at what you can accumulate in the long run. The table on page 162 shows that over the long term the cost of a daily cappuccino could add a year's salary to your retirement nest egg! Or, invest what you would otherwise spend on lottery tickets and guarantee a pot of gold for yourself. As for the saving made on cigarettes – well, I'll let the results speak for themselves.

	Weekly saving	Investment after 5 years	Investment after 10 years	Investment after 20 years
Weekly lotto ticket	$10	$3 110	$8 234	$30 594
Daily cappuccino	$18	$5 597	$14 821	$55 068
Weekly takeaway	$25	$7 774	$20 585	$76 484
Daily pack of cigarettes	$45	$13 993	$37 054	$137 671

Assumes reinvestment of income and 10% annual earnings, which is possible with quality growth investments.

I reckon that most of us can put aside just a few dollars a day without feeling the pinch too badly. And with the average age of divorce being around 40, most people still have around 20 years' worth of working life in which to build their wealth.

One type of high-yield bank account that is well worth a look are the online bank accounts or 'e-accounts' offered by a growing number of organisations, including ING, AMP, HSBC and St George Bank via Dragon Direct. These accounts need to be linked to a 'bricks and mortar' (traditional) bank account and you'll incur hefty penalties if you need face-to-face assistance, but on the plus side they have low, or no, fees, pay high interest on the full balance and your funds are at call.

Set some saving goals

The great thing about building your wealth is that you only need to kick a few financial goals and you'll be well on your way. People who are successful with money get used to the success and expect to succeed. This is a very powerful way of thinking. Of course, if you have no experience of managing your money or investing, it may not be too bright to expect to be a millionaire next year. Sure, I'm happy if your goal is to be a millionaire some way down the track, but you need to *learn* to be successful.

So, set some short-term goals. Plan to save $20 or $50 this week and give yourself a pat on the back when you do it. Then plan to save $100 or $200 this month. Give yourself some medium-term goals too. For example, you might say, 'Now I have learned to save, I'm going to get rid of my credit card bills by June'. But remember to give yourself a break. If you've achieved some goals and you continue to save, maybe you should allow yourself to take the holiday you've been planning for years but couldn't afford.

Following a divorce or separation, it is possible you may be making your own investment decisions for the first time. Centrelink provide a Financial Information Service (FIS), designed to help you understand how investments work. They also run seminars and can be contacted on 132 300.

Invest for the long term

Single parents in particular should be looking at two distinct strategies for two different times in your life: the child-raising years, and the years after children.

The child-raising years When the children are little, there is no doubt it can be very tough to get ahead, but you should be planning your finances with a view to being self-reliant. For women especially, the end of a relationship can also mean the end of time taken out of the workforce to raise a family. The right time to re-enter the workforce differs for everyone, and without the backup of a partner, life as a working parent can be tough. But if you've been out of the workforce for a while, I can't stress enough the importance of undertaking training or study to improve your employment prospects.

This is a key step. I know my mantra is 'save, save, save', but it's also important that you spend some money on your most important asset – you! Don't be frightened to dip into your pocket and invest in your own education and training. Do it now, so that further down the track you will become an employer's dream – a skilled, versatile and enthusiastic employee – and, best of all, your employer will pay you appropriately for it. Your ability to earn a higher income is one of your greatest assets, so do a course; gain new experiences; just do something to improve your 'employability', and your long-term financial independence. For more on studying, retraining and finding a job, take a look at Chapter 2 and Chapter 6.

My best advice for younger women re-entering the workforce is to save as much of your pay as possible. At this stage, superannuation need not be a priority. It is inflexible, you can't touch your money, and if your income is not very high the tax advantages are not that great. My advice is to try and get your foot in the real estate door. Save to buy a property either to live in, or as an investment.

Sure, it seems to be getting harder and harder to get your foot in the real estate door, with properties becoming more and more expensive. And many single parents and divorcees quite rightly wonder if they'll ever be able to afford a home of their own. But with planning and discipline it can be done.

First of all, approach a lender to see how much you can borrow on your income. A number of web sites (such as www.bank choice.com.au) have built-in calculators that let you work this out for yourself. The figure you come up with – called your 'borrowing limit' – may not be the most cheering reading you've ever come across, but it gives you a starting point.

A number of 'non-conforming' lenders specialise in providing loans to divorcees and other applicants sometimes rejected by mainstream lenders. The interest rates are generally higher – reflecting increased risk to the lender – but many borrowers start out with these loans and once they have established a decent credit record, they switch to cheaper, lower-interest lenders. For more on this, see Chapter 5.

Next, look at your budget to see how you can save for a deposit. Remember to allow an extra 5% on top of the purchase price of a property to cover things like stamp duty, legal fees, building inspections, and so on.

If the numbers look way beyond your reach, one alternative may be to buy a property with a friend or relative. This will expand your options, but make sure you put everything that you agree on in writing so that there is no basis for disputes any time down the track.

Real estate prices are very steep in many Australian cities, so you may need to broaden your search to outer suburbs or even rural areas where the prices are often lower. It also helps to be flexible about your choice of property. For example, a home unit is likely to be cheaper than a house, with the advantage that it is also easier to maintain.

After children Your financial plan should certainly keep going once the children are older. By this stage, hopefully you may be able to make extra repayments on the mortgage and even start thinking about other investments. If the tax advantages are worthwhile, that is, you are in a high enough tax bracket to make the difference between the super contribution rate (15%) and your marginal (top) income tax rate worthwhile, start putting extra money into super.

As you no doubt realise by now, the key to financial security is putting money away on a regular basis. That's how superannuation works best over many, many years and this is where women in particular are often at a disadvantage. Many women take time out of the workforce to have children and raise a family and often they don't make any super contributions for five, or even ten years. But once the children are older and you are able to get more fully back into the workforce, it is possible to focus on building a nest egg.

Let's assume, for example, that Sue is divorced and aged over 50. She kept the family home in her property settlement, she has no super but she earns around $35 000 annually and is willing to keep working for another ten years. On a tight budget, she can put $15 000 per year into super using salary sacrifice (making the contributions from her pre-tax salary), giving her a tidy nest egg in ten years' time. By selling her home and buying something smaller, Sue can have a comfortable retirement.

If you are unsure about salary sacrifice and what it involves, here's how it works. Instead of making contributions to your super fund out of your take-home pay, your employer makes the payments out of your gross (before tax) salary, so you pay income tax on the reduced amount. It may seem a big ask for our hypothetical divorcee Sue to make super contributions of $15 000 out of an annual salary of $35 000, but the table below shows that by using salary sacrifice she will be $4725 *better off* than if her super contribution is made from her after-tax salary.

Cash benefit from superannuation salary sacrifice

	Without salary sacrifice	With salary sacrifice
Gross salary	$35 000	$35 000
Less super contribution	$0	$15 000
Taxable salary	$35 000	$20 000
Less tax and Medicare	$7 405	$2 680
Less super contribution	$15 000	$0
Net cash salary	$12 595	$17 320
Cash gain from salary sacrifice		$4 725

Many super funds also offer low-cost death and total and permanent disability insurance as part of your membership. Some even offer low-interest housing loans and other discounts to low-income earners.

Make a will

A will is a legal document that sets out what you want done with your property and possessions after your death. If you die without a will (called dying 'intestate') or if your will is out of date, your estate can be distributed by a court-appointed administrator according to state laws and it is unlikely that this distribution will be in accordance with what you would have wanted – possibly even ending up in the government's coffers. If you need an incentive to draw up a will, consider this example of just how dreadful the consequences can be if you do not have one.

Let's assume that a 45-year-old divorced male with three children is killed in a car crash along with his 35-year-old female de facto partner. His estate is worth $250 000, but neither of them have a will. The couple live in NSW, so it is handled under the probate law of that state. Because the man is older than his partner, NSW law presumes he died first, and stipulates the first $150 000 of his estate plus 50% of the remainder (a total of $200 000) goes to his de facto's estate. That leaves only $50 000 for his children.

But, as his de facto is also intestate, her estate, now including the $200 000 from her partner's estate, will go to *her* next of kin. This could include any children by a previous partner, her parents, siblings, an uncle or an aunt; even a psychopathic cousin. In the worst possible case, if his de facto has no relatives, the estate ends up going to the state government. What an appalling result, considering he has three children of his own who get under $17 000 each, less legal fees.

If you need further convincing, remember that without a will the administration of your estate becomes not just more difficult, but more expensive.

I look at making a will in more detail in Chapter 9, but it is worth pointing out that your will should be updated every five years or if your situation changes, especially through separation or divorce. An existing will can be rendered invalid if you remarry.

SEPARATION SURVIVAL TIPS

- Seek expert independent advice from a solicitor as soon as possible, preferably before you separate.
- The arrangements you put in place for the kids at the time you separate are likely to be continued by the court if there is a dispute later on, unless there is a very significant reason why they should be changed. So put in place an arrangement you can live with right from the start.
- Reach an agreement about child support if possible, but if you can't, lodge an application with the Child Support Agency without delay. It could take some time for the agency to work out an agreement.
- If you cannot agree on a property settlement, the Family Court can take about a year to hear your application, and sometimes longer. Consider mediation as a low-cost option.

Useful contacts

	Telephone	Web site
Centrelink	131 021	www.centrelink.gov.au
Child Care Access Hotline	1800 670 305	
Child Support Agency	131 272	www.csa.gov.au
Department of Family and Community Services	1300 653 227	www.facs.gov.au
Family Assistance Office	136 150	www.familyassist.gov.au
Family Court of Australia	Adelaide: 08 8205 2666	www.familycourt.gov.au
	Brisbane: 07 3248 2200	
	Canberra: 02 6267 0511	
	Darwin: 08 8981 1488	
	Hobart: 03 6232 1725	
	Melbourne: 03 8600 3777	
	Perth: 08 9224 8222	
	Sydney: 02 9217 7111	
	After hours emergency: 1800 622 395	

9

Retirement

In the early 1980s, I used to do a talkback radio segment on Sydney radio, and one of the issues that always came up was retirement. In those days, the majority of callers planned to retire at 65 and their financial planning was pretty haphazard, often taking place *after* retirement.

How things have changed! These days, we often retire earlier and in much better health. We are living much longer, so we can expect to spend far more time in retirement. In fact, the average 55-year-old is likely to be around for another quarter of a century, so many of us will now spend almost as much time in retirement as we did in the workforce.

But it's not just about living longer – we are also retiring earlier. Currently, less than 25% of men work to age 65, and nearly one in five retirees is younger than 54. We also have different expectations as to how our time will be filled. The days when the elderly were expected to see out their days playing bingo or minding the grandchildren are thankfully a thing of the past. Today we look on retirement as the stage in our lives when we can enjoy all those things we may not have had time for when we were younger, like travel, golf, hobbies and socialising.

WHEN CAN I RETIRE?

In Australia there is no age when you *must* retire (although certain occupations may impose age limits), so if you are willing and able to do so, there may be nothing to stop you working well into your nineties! Some people retire at 55, the age at which they can access their super. For others, though, their retirement age depends on their ability to access the age pension. For men that's at age 65, and for women it's currently at age 62, however this is being progressively increased so that by July 2013, women will also need to be 65 to be eligible for the pension.

The government increasingly expects us to fund our own retirement, and with good reason. The Australian population is ageing. The Australian Institute of Health and Welfare reckons that in just 20 years one in five people will be aged over 65, with the over-85s making up almost 3% of the population. And one report I read stated that for each couple then aged 65, one of them has a one in three chance of making it to 100! So, it's not too hard to see that there just won't be sufficient taxpayers to foot the aged-pension bill.

CAN I AFFORD TO RETIRE?

Retirement dreams of golf, sport and travel are great, but unfortunately they involve a substance few of us have enough of – money. Sure, most of us won't see out our days cruising the world, but the good news is that, with careful planning, it's possible to enjoy a decent lifestyle in retirement for a lot less than you earned during your days in the workforce. That's partly because senior Australians get the benefit of some pretty handy tax breaks (see the section on tax and retirees on page 186), but also because many of the big costs we face before retirement no longer apply.

Take a look at the table on page 172, which compares two families: a couple in their 30s with two young children, whom we will call the Youngs, and a retired couple in their late 60s – the Oldes. The Youngs are a fairly traditional family in which only one partner works, but they enjoy a very good income of $90 000 per annum. The Oldes earn a far more modest income of $27 300 – around the national average for retired couples, but thanks to the way they structured their retirement investments together with the senior Australians tax offset (more on this later), they pay almost nothing in tax. The Youngs, on the other hand, lose a massive 34% of their gross income to tax.

The Youngs have a typical mortgage for a family of their size, but despite interest rates being among the lowest in decades, they still pay 23% – almost a quarter of their take-home pay – into the mortgage. The Oldes, on the other hand, paid off their mortgage long ago. And while the junior Youngs may be small, they make a man-sized dent in the family budget, chewing up a further 29% of the family's disposable income. In addition to making super contributions, the Youngs also have to pay for costs that are part of being in the workforce. The whole point of the exercise is to show how in our middle years, when we can have some pretty solid financial commitments, what sounds like a decent income can often be thinly stretched – especially as studies continually show that the more we earn, the more we spend. In retirement however, what sounds like a little has the potential to go a long way.

It is also likely that your spending habits will change as you get older. For example, the early to middle years of retirement are when your travel and recreation costs are highest. But, overall,

	The 'Youngs' – family with two children	The 'Oldes' – retired couple
Gross income	$	$
Salary	90 000	–
Pension plus investments	–	27 300*
Total income	**90 000**	**27 300**
Less income tax	31 000	–
Income after tax	**59 000**	**27 300**
Costs per annum		–
Mortgage	14 000+	–
Two children aged 5–9	17 500^	–
Cost of one person working full-time	2 600#	–
Super contributions	3 000	–
Total fixed costs	**37 100**	**–**
Funds left over	**23 400**	**27 300**

Figures are rounded.

*Average income for a retired couple, ABS Year Book Australia, 2002.

+Based on the average mortgage of $174 000 over 25 years for a couple with dependent children, ABS Cat 4130.0, October 1999. Interest calculated at 6.5%, giving monthly repayments of $1175.

^Based on the weekly cost of raising two children of $338 for a family on this level of gross income – 'The public and private costs of children', NATSEM, April 2000, www.natsem.canberra.edu.au.

#Costs of being in the workforce include fares to and from work, clothes for work and occasional take-away lunches. These costs are estimated here at $50 a week.

the amount you'll need to fund your retirement depends on the sort of lifestyle you're hoping for. Someone who intends to update their car every few years and dine out a couple of times a week will need a bigger nest egg than a couple who are prepared to share one car and live more modestly.

The challenge of retirement planning these days is that you are preparing for what will (hopefully) be the long term. The difficulty is that your situation may change along the way, and if past form is anything to go by, the government is almost certain to introduce new laws at some point along the way that will affect your entitlements. This is one reason I strongly urge retirees to seek competent professional advice when it comes to planning their retirement income.

Another reason that I recommend you get some decent financial planning is that retirement planning can be a very complex area of investing. The attitude of 'she'll be right mate' might be okay if you are thinking about buying a new pair of shoes, but when it comes to investing for your future, it's an approach that could leave you seriously out of pocket. Yes, good financial planning advice will cost you, but in many cases it could be some of the best money you will spend in retirement.

Now, telling you to go and see a good financial planner about retirement income does not mean I'm trying to sidestep the job of telling you about it myself: I'm still going to explain the ins and outs of how to make the most of your money in retirement. But what I want to point out upfront is that the best way to use the information in this chapter is to read it *before* you see a financial adviser, so that you've got the groundwork in place to help you understand your options. Then maybe you can look over the chapter again after you've received some professional advice, to help make sense of it all.

WHAT SORT OF INCOME CAN I EXPECT?

One of the nice things about our society is that if, through health or choice, you want to be fully retired and you have no assets, a man at age 65 and a woman at age 62 may be entitled to an age pension. And, according to the Australian Bureau of Statistics (ABS), government pensions are the main source of income for about 75% of the over-65s. This is expected to continue for some time, so let's take a look at the age pension first, followed by super and retirement income streams.

The age pension

The age pension is reviewed several times a year, but at March 2003 it was set at $440 per fortnight for singles and $367 (each) for couples. But you do not become automatically eligible once you leave the workforce.

There are two tests that are used to decide the amount of the pension you are entitled to. One test looks at your assets and the other looks at your income. Centrelink, the government agency responsible for social security payments, compares the pensions that you would be entitled to under both these tests and pays you whichever is the smaller amount.

In simple terms, the greater your income and/or assets are, the lower your age pension is likely to be, if indeed you receive one at all.

The income test Under this test, a couple is allowed a full pension if they earn less than $204 a fortnight. For every dollar you earn over this amount, the pension you are entitled to drops by 40 cents. 'Income' includes money received from employment as well as returns on your investments. Note that there are 'deeming' rules (see page 175), which mean your investments are assumed to earn a minimum amount irrespective of how much they actually do earn, and Centrelink takes this into account when it works out your total income.

The assets test This test looks at the value of your assets, although different limits apply depending on whether or not you own your home. If your assets exceed the limit (the March 2003 figures are set out at the end of this chapter), your fortnightly pension is reduced by $3 for every $1000 they exceed the threshold.

'Assets' covers an enormous range of things, including most home contents, cars, boats, rental properties, holiday houses, and the value of financial investments like shares and term deposits. Centrelink values your assets at market value (what you would get if you sold them), less any debt still owing on them. Some assets are not included in the test, and for most people this will include the family home if you live in it, and possibly any 'complying pensions' you may have, which I'll talk about later.

Even if you're not eligible for the full pension, it's still worth applying for a part pension as this makes you eligible for a Pensioner Concession Card which gives you access to a range of discounts (see page 191).

Deeming

Retirement is the time when work stops for you, but it starts in earnest for your assets. And this is especially important given the government's rules on 'deeming'. Deeming was introduced in 1991 to discourage retirees from putting all their money into low or zero-interest savings accounts. It simply means that the government deems, or assumes, that your financial investments (which cover almost every conceivable type of investment) have earned a certain amount of income for the year, regardless of their actual return. Centrelink then takes this amount into account when they work out your eligibility for the pension under the income test.

Deeming rates are reviewed from time to time but, at present, the first $34 400 of a single person's investments and the first $57 400 of a couple's investments will be deemed to have earned income at a rate of 2.5% per annum. Amounts over these limits are deemed to earn a 4% annual return.

Most banks offer saving accounts that are marketed as pensioner deeming accounts because they pay these tiered interest rates. But I reckon you're much better off placing any cash you don't need for day-to-day expenses into other at-call investments (like, say, a cash management account), where you stand to earn more than the miserly deeming rate.

An information leaflet on the factors you should consider when choosing a deeming account is available from Centrelink by phoning 132 300.

Gifting

It can be tempting for retirees to give their children or grandchildren a head-start in life by giving cash or other assets away to them. This is generous, but it could leave you in financial hot water.

Under the government's 'gifting laws', if you give away assets valued at more than $10 000 in any 'year' (that's the financial year, from 1 July to 30 June), your pension may be affected. Any amounts over $10 000 that you give away are treated by Centrelink as money still in your bank account for five years from the date of the gift, including it in both the income and assets test. The limit of $10 000 applies whether you are single or a couple. Since July 2002, the $10 000 annual limit still applies, but the most you can give away over a five-year period without affecting your pension is $30 000.

Other payments you may be eligible for

Veterans' payments If you were a member of the Australian Defence Force, you may also be eligible for a service pension through the Department of Veteran's Affairs (DVA).

Rent assistance If you are a pensioner and renting privately you may be eligible for rent assistance. The amount you get will depend on the rent you pay and your family situation – whether you are single, married, have children with you or share with other people.

Centrelink Pension Loan Scheme This may not be everyone's cup of tea, but if you own your own home and you are willing to use it as security for a loan, you may be eligible for Centrelink's Pension Loan Scheme.

Under this scheme, you can take out a loan with Centrelink where you will be paid a fortnightly amount (equal to the age pension of $440 for singles and $734 for couples). If you are on a part pension, you can borrow an amount to take you up to the full pension. So, for example, a retired single person who receives a pension payment of $200 may be able to borrow an extra $240 per fortnight.

The amount that you are eligible for will depend on the value of your home, which is used as security for the loan. The loan is not paid off until you die, the interest rate is quite low (5.25% per annum as at February 2003) and the payments can be discontinued at any time. The only real downside for cash-strapped pensioners is that you may leave a smaller estate than would otherwise be the case, but this has to be better than living an impoverished existence.

To be eligible for the scheme, you or your partner need to be of pension age (65 for men and 62 for women) and eligible for at least a part pension.

I'm certainly not going to pretend that the age pension will fund many people's dream lifestyle. It won't. It's fixed by law at 25% of male average weekly earnings, which is well below the technical poverty line. You will be unlikely to be drinking champagne and eating lobster, but take heart that if this is the worst-case scenario, everything else gets better.

SUPERANNUATION AND RETIREES

When it comes to super, retirees have three main options. You can choose between:

- taking your super as a lump sum and investing it yourself
- investing in a 'retirement income stream', or
- a combination of the above.

Taking a lump sum

There's no doubt that a lump sum is handy for retirees who have large amounts of debt (like a mortgage) that they wish to pay off, or who are looking to take a big trip or buy a new car. But if you opt for a lump sum with the intention of managing your own investment portfolio, think carefully. Firstly, it's something I would only recommend to people with a fair bit of investment experience. And, secondly, if you invest your super in, say, shares, property or a term deposit, not only will these amounts be included in the assets and income test for the age pension, you will probably pay tax on the income they earn at normal personal tax rates. This may not be the case with other types of investments, which may offer tax concessions (see page 179 – 'Retirement income streams').

On top of this, our government believes (probably correctly) that if we take our super as a lump sum we are more likely to blow it than if we have a formal payment arrangement which distributes income periodically. And when you think that your money may have to last 20 years or more, it's probably not bad reasoning. So, to discourage Australians from taking out their super in one hit, lump sum payments attract some very heavy tax rates.

If you're over 55, for example, you'll have to include 5% of any pre-July 1983 super component in your assessable income. If you have over $112 405 (2003 rate, indexed annually) in post-June 1983 contributions you'll be taxed at around 15% on the excess, plus the Medicare levy of 1.5%. There is also the spectre of what's known as your 'Reasonable Benefits Limit' (RBL). This is the most that the government lets you accumulate in your super while still enjoying concessional tax rates.

We all have two RBLs, and the one that applies depends on how we use our super nest egg. If you take your super as a lump sum or as an 'allocated pension' (I'll explain these soon but let's just say it's a retirement investment that pays you a steady income), you face the 'lump sum' RBL of $562 195 (for 2002/03). However, if you use your money to buy what's called a 'complying pension' (this is described on page 184) you get a 'pension' RBL, which at $1 124 384 (for 2002/03) is far more generous. If you accumulate more than your RBL, the excess is taxed at 48.5% when you withdraw it. The fact is that only around 10% of retirees have the 'problem' of having more than $560 000 in super, but regardless of this, most retirees very sensibly shy away from taking their super as a lump sum.

Retirement income streams

One of the big challenges many retirees face is going from receiving a regular weekly wage or salary to having to arrange your own income and making sure that it, too, is regular. One way of achieving this is to invest your super in a 'private' pension.

What you are doing here is exchanging your lump sum for a series of regular income payments. The payments you receive are a combination of your own capital (your 'drawdowns') plus whatever returns your capital earns. There are various types of pensions, but for most retirees the important distinction is whether a pension is 'complying' (age-pension friendly) or non-complying. Non-complying pensions, in particular, 'allocated' pensions, are the most popular type of private pension among retirees, so I'll take a look at these first.

Allocated pensions Allocated pensions are a bit like a managed fund where you invest money with a financial institution such as AMP, AXA or MLC. They then invest the money in the underlying assets of your choice. For example, you can opt for a 'conservative' pension fund investing mainly in cash-based securities, or you can choose a 'growth' fund with an emphasis on shares and property. Alternatively, you may prefer a 'balanced' fund with investments spread across a broad range of assets. Like a managed fund, you pay an annual management fee – usually around 1.5% of the value of your funds under management.

For each year that you have your money invested in the allocated pension, you choose the size of your annual payments within maximum and minimum limits. These limits are calculated by the government, based on your life expectancy, and they are designed to encourage you to draw down sufficient money so that you have a reasonable retirement lifestyle, without spending your nest egg too quickly.

There are some real advantages to allocated pensions. As you have a say in the underlying investments, you get to share in the spoils if a particular investment market takes off (although the flipside to this is that the value of your capital can fall if the market drops). You also have the flexibility to 'commute' all or part of your pension fund, which simply means you can withdraw lump sums from it. This is very reassuring as it gives you access to emergency funds should you need them. And the flexibility of allocated pensions even extends to the hereafter, since in the event of your death, the balance of your account goes to your estate.

All these benefits pale into comparison, however, with the tax advantages of allocated pensions. To begin with, when you roll your super into an allocated pension, no lump sum tax is payable. And while the income you receive is taxed at your marginal (top) rate of tax, you are usually allowed a 15% tax rebate on this income (take a look at how this works on page 181). Rebates are amounts that are taken off your tax bill, and they are meant to compensate retirees for the 15% tax imposed on super contributions and fund earnings.

On top of this rebate, you may also be entitled to a 'deductible' amount if you contributed money to your super from your after-tax income (in other words, you made super contributions that you didn't claim a tax deduction for). These 'undeducted contributions' are paid back to you over the life of the pension as part of your annual pension payments. As the taxman treats these amounts as a return of your own savings, they are not included in your assessable income. There's no need to be concerned about calculating all this – the manager of your pension plan should work it all out – but the bottom line is that you pay less tax.

It all sounds very complicated, but the main point is that the combination of the tax-free amount and the tax rebate mean that you get a larger disposable income. In fact, using an allocated pension, a single retiree can earn around $30 000 a year tax-free, while couples can earn just over $50 000 (combined) before they pay tax.

Here's how. Let's say that Don, a 65-year-old single retiree, invests $300 000 in an allocated pension. Of this amount, $100 000 comes from undeducted contributions (remember, those are the contributions Don made to his super fund with his *after-tax* money, for which he didn't claim a deduction). Don opts to receive a yearly income from his allocated pension of $35 000.

As Don made undeducted contributions to his nest egg, part of his annual pension payment will be tax-free. Each year this amount will equal the value of Don's undeducted contributions divided by his life expectancy (around 16 years for a 65-year-old). So, in his case, $6169 of his annual pension payment (being $100 000 divided by his life expectancy) is tax-free.

That leaves him with taxable income of $28 831 ($35 000 – $6169). The tax bill on this would normally be $5029, but Don gets a 15% allocated pension rebate of $4325 ($28 831 × 15%). On top of this, he can also claim a senior Australians tax offset of $1126 (see page 187). This brings his total rebates to $5451. As this is more than his tax bill of $5029, he'll pay no income tax at all, although he still pays the Medicare levy of $432 ($28 831 × 1.5%).

The tax advantages are a real point in favour of allocated pensions, but it's not all beer and skittles. The first downside is that the income from your pension is not guaranteed. You will receive a payment while there is money in your account, but, as you'll see below, this could run out.

How long will my allocated pension last? With allocated pensions, the payments you receive reduce your nest egg, and the investment returns increase it. So the issue of how long your money will last basically depends on two things: the size of your regular pension payments and the returns your money earns.

I pointed out earlier that the size of your annual pension payment must be within maximum and minimum guidelines, and this is one area where retirees can directly impact on how long their money will last. Unless you have a pretty big nest egg, you need to find the lowest amount you can draw down while still enjoying a decent retirement lifestyle.

You also have some say in the returns your money earns, when you select the underlying investments of the pension plan. If you put all your money into a conservative plan, you can expect steady income returns but very little capital growth. Without capital growth, inflation can eat away at the purchasing power of your nest egg. This puts pressure on you to draw down increasing amounts of capital, thereby whittling your money away prematurely.

The table below shows how long your money will last in an allocated pension for different annual returns and at different rates of capital draw-down. Let's say that you want your pension payment set at 6% of your capital. If you invest in a conservative pension plan with an annual return of 4%, your money will last around 19 years. Alternatively, you could invest in a balanced pension plan,

Number of years an allocated income stream will last for

Annual return on investment	Income set at 5% of capital	Income set at 6% of capital	Income set at 7% of capital	Income set at 8% of capital
4%	24 years	19 years	16 years	14 years
6%	33 years	24 years	19 years	16 years
8%	Indefinitely	36 years	25 years	20 years
10%	Indefinitely	Indefinitely	52 years	27 years

Source: ipac securities. Assumes the draw down increases by 2.5% each year.

earning, say, 6% per annum, and your money will last for around 24 years. However, if you opt for a growth-focused fund, earning 8% annually, your capital is generating more in returns than you are taking out, so the money should last indefinitely.

Looking at the table on page 182, it would be easy to assume that the way to make your retirement money last is to invest everything in a growth-based pension. But there's a catch. Returns on allocated pension funds generally reflect the performance of the underlying investments. So, for example, if you invest in an allocated pension fund where the underlying assets are shares, if the share market takes a tumble, the value of your investment, and your returns, could also fall.

So, what's the answer? Well, it comes down to having a diversified portfolio where your income comes from a range of sources including, say, interest-bearing deposits and shares as well as a private pension. Ideally you should aim to have around two or three years' worth of income invested in low-risk assets like cash and fixed interest. That way you don't have to draw on your growth assets in periods when the market is down, thereby turning a 'paper' loss into a real one. Then, in the good years, you can top up these conservative investments with the gains you've made on your growth assets.

Spreading your money between conservative and growth pension plans will help make your money last, but the fact is that many plans require a minimum investment of $10 000 to $20 000, so unless you've got a large amount to invest, it can be easier said than done. If you have a moderately small amount of capital, say $100 000 or less, your number one priority should be protecting the value of your capital, so stick with more conservative investments.

Something else you need to be aware of with allocated pensions is that they are 'non-complying'. This simply means that the value of your capital and part of the income is included in the tests used by Centrelink when it determines your eligibility for the age pension. The part of the pension payment you receive that is a return of your own capital is excluded from the income test. But the full value of the amount you invested in the pension plan will be taken into account in the assets test.

Complying pensions The other type of retirement income stream is 'complying' pensions or annuities (I'll stick with the term 'annuities' here, to avoid confusion with the age pension). You may also see these investments described as 'age-pension friendly' because they get favourable treatment under the social security rules. There are basically two types of complying annuities: lifetime annuities and life expectancy annuities.

Lifetime annuities As the name suggests, with a lifetime annuity you'll be paid on a regular basis (you can usually opt to be paid monthly, quarterly or annually) for the rest of your life. The amount you receive each year is fixed when you take out the annuity. This is great if you're in good health as you get a guaranteed income for life. It also makes budgeting and financial planning much easier, and you don't have to worry about what's happening in investment markets as your income is fixed upfront. And you can nominate a 'reversionary' beneficiary, which means that if you die, the annuity payments pass to the person you've nominated (your beneficiary). As a rule, though, they'll receive a proportion of your payments, not the full amount.

Life expectancy annuities These annuities pay you an income for a fixed period, which is generally in line with your life expectancy. Remember, though, that the life expectancy figures produced by the government are averages – you may well live longer than the statistics suggest. This is important because while it's great to live longer than expected, you could outlast your annuity and find yourself relying solely on the age pension.

Unlike allocated pensions where *you* bear the risk of your money running out, with both types of complying annuities the financial institution offering them bears the risk. Basically, the super company or life office commits to paying you an agreed income either until you die, in the case of a lifetime annuity, or for a specified term in the case of a life expectancy annuity. To minimise their risk, the fund manager (who decides the underlying investments) generally chooses lower-risk investments, which do not generate high returns.

And, once you have invested your money in a complying annuity, your yearly income generally won't vary by much. You can opt for your annual income to be increased either by a small annual percentage or for changes in the cost of living, but these changes are usually modest. So, even if investment markets are booming, your income won't change to reflect this. The flipside is that if investment markets fall, you have the security of knowing that your income remains the same.

One other aspect to be aware of is that most life expectancy pensions do not let you 'commute' or get access to your capital. In other words, you cannot withdraw large amounts of the money you have invested in the pension fund. So, if you are interested in this type of investment, it is important to have part of your money invested in other assets (such as a cash management account) that you can easily get hold of for the times when you need emergency funds to pay for things like repairs to your home.

So, complying annuities offer security on one hand but inflexibility on the other. Yes, you get a bigger RBL if you roll part of your super into a complying annuity rather than a non-complying one (see page 178 – 'Taking a lump sum'), but for most ordinary Australians this is not a big drawcard. The thing that has made life expectancy and lifetime annuities attractive to retirees is that they are 'age-pension friendly'. This means that the principal you invest in a complying annuity is exempt from the Centrelink assets test, and part of your yearly annuity payment (the amount that is a return of your own principal) is exempt from the income test.

In a nutshell, this means that for every $10 000 you invest in a complying pension (up to the assets test limit), you can increase your fortnightly age pension by $30 (assuming you are eligible for the age pension in every other respect). That's an additional age pension payment of $780 each year, which has the effect of boosting the overall returns from these annuities, without increasing the risk.

Here's how it works. Let's say, for example, that Gwen, a single retiree, meets all the basic requirements for the age pension (most notably, she's an Australian resident and she's over 62), but her assets are valued at $294 000, which is right on the assets limit for a person in her position (single, homeowner), so she doesn't even qualify for a part age pension. She decides to invest $10 000 in a life expectancy annuity. This takes her assets to $284 000, which is below the Centrelink assets test level, and she becomes eligible for a part age pension of about $780 annually. This is on top of the earnings from her complying pension, so it's like getting an extra 7.8% return on her investment, which is not bad. The icing on the cake is that as a part-pensioner, Gwen is now entitled to a Pensioner Concession Card, which makes her eligible for a range of discounts (see page 191).

You've probably realised at this point that like many aspects of retirement income, the social security and income tax rules surrounding annuities and private pensions are complex, so you really do have to get expert professional advice. Once again it comes back to my earlier recommendation that you really need to speak with a trusted financial adviser or accountant.

TAX AND RETIREES

Although the age pension is a taxable payment, most aged pensioners don't pay tax thanks to the low income tax offset and the senior Australians tax offset. Don't be put off by the term 'offset'; it's the name given to rebates these days, and the important thing you need to know about them is that they reduce the amount of tax you have to pay.

Senior Australians tax offset

To receive this offset you need to be over 65 if you're a man, or over 62 if you are a woman, be eligible for the age pension and, rather oddly, you'll need to have been out of jail for the entire income year. The amount you can claim as an offset depends on your income and marital status, but as a guide, the senior's offset reduces by 12.5 cents for every dollar you earn over $20000, cutting out altogether when your annual income reaches $37840 (indexed).

A single person, for example, with a taxable income of $20000 would normally have a tax bill of $2380. But this tax bill will be reduced to nil by the combination of the senior Australians tax offset of $2230 plus the low income tax offset of $150 (see below). You don't have to work out your rebate – the tax office will do it for you. One of the pluses of the senior Australians tax offset is that any unused rebate from one partner can be added to the rebate of the other partner to reduce their tax bill.

Low income tax offset

If your annual income is below $24450, you can claim a low income tax offset. Where your income is less than $20700 you can claim the full offset of $150, and the offset reduces by four cents for each dollar you earn over this amount, cutting out altogether at $24450.

Medicare

The Medicare levy threshold is currently $20000 for people who are eligible for the senior Australians tax offset. So, if you earn below $20000 you pay no levy. If your taxable income is over $20000,

Medicare is levied at the normal rate of 1.5% of your taxable income.

MAXIMISING YOUR RETIREMENT INCOME

Get good advice – early

From a financial perspective, retirement is the time when most of us are likely to need advice. Hopefully having spent decades building up three key pools of wealth (your home, your super and other investment assets), the decisions made at this stage of life are critical. When income is still coming in mistakes are of a lesser importance because you are not generally relying on income from your assets. But once full-time work stops and you start relying on your assets, it is really important that you get your investment and tax strategies spot on.

If you are happy to devote some time to researching and closely monitoring your investments, it can be fun to manage your own portfolio in retirement. Of course, you'll need to keep detailed records and have a pretty good grasp of the investment market, but the do-it-yourself approach can work.

Realistically, though, most people recognise that they're not budding funds managers and appreciate they will need at least some professional help to manage their money. These days it isn't enough to just know a balanced fund from a blue chip share. Our complex tax system is a minefield for retirees, with serious issues like capital gains tax, franked dividends, lump sum tax, and so on.

Now, while most retirees sensibly choose to get some professional help, it's still important that you understand the strategy being used for your investments, the level of risk involved and the sort of potential long-term returns you can expect.

As you head towards retirement, look for a competent adviser whom you trust and feel comfortable with. In my experience, it is best to look for an adviser who can offer a simplified investment portfolio with a clear reporting system. As always, if you are unclear about anything your adviser discusses, do not be afraid to ask questions.

The National Information Centre on Retirement Investments offers a free, independent information service for retirees with a modest nest egg. They do not give financial planning advice, but they can provide you with plenty of free information. Their number is 1800 020 110, and their web site is at www.nicri.org.au.

If you are looking for a financial adviser, the Financial Planning Association (FPA) can put you in touch with someone suitable. The web site for the FPA is at www.fpa.asn.au, and below is a list of contact telephone numbers for each state.

Financial Planning Association offices

Australian Capital Territory	(02) 6260 4567
New South Wales	1800 815 168 / (02) 9223 0900
Queensland	(07) 3839 2427
South Australia	(08) 8291 8522
Tasmania	(03) 6224 8855
Victoria	1800 626 393 / (03) 9627 5299
Western Australia	(08) 9486 1788

Diversify your investments

One important piece of advice I can give you is not to do what previous generations would have done and put all or most of your assets into cash and fixed-interest investments in the early part of your retirement. This may have been a sensible strategy for past generations where a 65-year-old had a six-year life expectancy, but for today's 55- or 60-year-old with a 20-year-plus life expectancy, it's downright silly. With such a long-term life horizon, a strong exposure to growth assets, such as property or shares, is vital. Sure, your capital will fall in value in the bad years, but over 20 years you need your capital to grow in value to keep pace with inflation and also your income. This is the long-term advantage of quality property and share investments. Not only can their value rise with inflation over time, but so too can the income you receive, and that's why many retirees need a diversified portfolio with exposure to both higher-risk, capital growth generating assets like shares and property, as well as more traditional low-risk, income generating investments.

The question of just which growth assets are right for you is a highly personal one which can really only be answered by a financial adviser who takes into account things like your age, how you feel about risk, and the overall size of your nest egg. So, while I can't talk in specifics, what I can say is that young retirees in particular really need to include growth investments in their portfolio to protect the value of their long-term wealth.

Be aware of your entitlements

Retirees not currently receiving a pension should check to see what they are eligible for. Even with a part-pension as low as $1 a week, you could qualify for benefits worth quite a bit each year from:

- travel concessions
- cheaper pharmaceuticals
- reduced council and water rates, and
- reduced telephone charges.

Unfortunately, lots of independent retirees feel the pension is a charity, but it's not. You have paid your taxes for decades and you have a right to get some back.

Make use of discount cards It's rare to get something for nothing, but here's some good news about three cards that will save you money.

- **Pensioner Concession Card** – this entitles pensioners to a quarterly telephone allowance of about $19, and cheaper medicines (where they are listed on the Pharmaceutical Benefits Scheme). Other benefits will be available depending on your home state, ranging from reductions in your council and water rates, gas and electricity bills to reduced public transport fares. To apply for a Pensioner Concession Card contact Centrelink on 132 300.

- **Commonwealth Seniors Health Card (CSHC)** – this card is available to people of pension age, but who are not eligible for the pension. You need to meet an income test to qualify (see the table at the end of this chapter). This card also entitles you to a quarterly telephone allowance, plus discounts on some medicines. For more information contact Centrelink on 132 300 or the Department of Veterans' Affairs on 133 254.

- **Seniors Card** – the Seniors Card is not a pensioner's card, it is a retail discount and travel concession card offered to elderly Australians. It is not means tested, and although the criteria for eligibility for the card differs between states, you generally need to be aged over 60 and working less than 20 hours a week.

  I've come across figures that suggest a Seniors Card can save you around $8 each week or $400 a year, but many retirees tell me they flash their card just about everywhere and they generally get a discount. Contact details to apply for a Seniors Card can be found on the web site at www.seniorscard.com.au, or see the table on page 192 for the phone numbers in each state.

Contact numbers for Seniors Card information

Australian Capital Territory	(02) 6282 3777
New South Wales	1300 364 758
Northern Territory	1800 777 704
Queensland	(07) 3224 2788
	1800 175 500 (country callers)
South Australia	(08) 8226 6852
Tasmania	(03) 6222 7651
Victoria	(03) 9616 8241
Western Australia	(08) 9220 1111

Work for as long as you can

Work is more than just a source of income – it can provide important social and intellectual stimulation. Of course, not everyone wants to keep working, but if you can, it shortens the period on which you will be relying on your savings and extends the time you can add to your nest egg.

As a sweetener to encourage us to work beyond pension age, the government has introduced the Pension Bonus Scheme. This is a tax-free lump sum bonus, designed to encourage older Australians to remain in the workforce (and so put off claiming the pension).

To receive the bonus, you need to register with Centrelink, and then continue working 960 hours in a year, for at least 12 months. This is an average of 20 hours a week, but the time can be made up in any way. The bonus starts off small at just over $1000 for the first year you continue working, but if you remain in the workforce for an additional five years, the bonus rises to a handy $26 236 (2002/03 singles rate). You can claim it when you finally retire, but remember you need to be eligible for the age pension to receive it.

Don't feel you have to leave it all to the kids

Whether you are currently retired or hoping to exit the workforce in a few years, something that you should work out sooner rather than later is how much you intend to leave behind for your beneficiaries. Bear in mind that the more you leave behind, the less you have to spend on yourself. In Australia, many retirees still feel it is important to leave a decent estate for their children, and while that is a personal decision, I would hate to see the situation where people are living a hand-to-mouth existence simply to provide for their (usually) adult children. Look after yourself first. If there's something left over for the kids, all good and well.

> Think twice before you act as guarantor for the debts of other people – including your own children. You could end up losing everything – even your home, if things go wrong.

Avoid the 'asset rich/cash poor' trap

Ask a pensioner how much equity they have in their home, and most could tell you 'everything between the rugs and the rafters'. Now while many of us aspire to this, for seniors it can be a real problem. You see, many retirees are house rich but cash poor. The family home remains the single most important asset for the over-55s, accounting for around half of the wealth of the average 65-year-old. Bank deposits are the second most-favoured asset which, like the family home, offer great security but not huge opportunities for income. The family home in particular not only locks up large amounts of retirement capital, it often proves a drain, making increasing demands on your time and money for repairs and maintenance.

The good news is that thanks to rising house prices over the last decade (particularly in metropolitan areas), many retirees are sitting on (or in) a pretty substantial asset. Now, I realise the family home often has significant sentimental value, but there aren't too many of us who can afford to have substantial amounts of money tied up in an asset which produces no income. Yet that's just what many older Australians do.

Consider this: one retired couple who came to me for advice on how to increase their income were living in the family home in suburban Sydney. The property, which they had purchased for $67 000 in 1974, held great sentimental value, but was increasingly in need of repairs and maintenance. Their children were married with families of their own and the couple was 'tired of cleaning a pool that no one swims in'. The house was put on the market, and it sold for $525 000. As the family home is exempt from capital gains tax, the full amount was tax-free. The couple purchased a two-bedroom unit in a nearby suburb for $275 000, pocketing over $200 000 after meeting the various costs of buying and selling. Any doubts they may have had about farewelling the family home were quickly overcome in the excitement of the South Pacific cruise they treated themselves to, courtesy of their new nest egg.

The same 'make all your assets work for you' principle can be applied to holiday homes and other non-income-producing assets. It might mean you leave less to your estate, but it will certainly improve your retirement lifestyle.

Selling the family home will appeal to some retirees, but it is not for everyone. In the circumstances where you simply do not want to sell up and move, it may be worthwhile to consider a product known as a 'reverse mortgage'.

Most of us are familiar with the standard, run-of-the-millstone mortgage, which is more correctly called a 'forward mortgage', though hardly anyone ever uses this term. These are the normal loans used to fund the purchase of a home, usually over a long term, with repayments made up of a combination of principal and interest. The property is used as security, and at the end of the loan term – seemingly halfway through the millennium – there is no debt remaining and the property is all yours.

In the case of a 'reverse' mortgage, the opposite happens. The equity you have in your home is converted into cash, either through the payment of a lump sum, or through a monthly annuity. The home owner receives payments rather than making them, so over time the mortgage debt increases rather than decreases. And as the loan balance builds up, the amount of equity you have in your home is reduced.

The loan is paid out either when you die or if you choose to sell your home, at which point the sale proceeds go to repaying the debt. The big downside here of course is that interest is charged on the growing balance, and over time the effect of compounding interest begins to work against you, with the interest becoming an increasingly large part of the amount owed.

Now, a variety of products based on the concept of reverse mortgages have been available at various times in Australia, though most have gone the way of the Tasmanian tiger. However, in December 2002, St George Bank introduced a reverse mortgage, marketed as a 'Seniors Access Home Loan'. With this loan, customers aged 65 to 69 can borrow up to $80 000 or 15% of the value of their property (whichever is lower), and homeowners aged 70 or over can borrow the lesser of $100 000 or 20% of the property's value. With this particular product, St George will absorb any shortfall should the loan balance exceed the proceeds from the sale of the home.

It can be something of a wake-up call to find at age 65 that your life expectancy is around 14 years and your investments are only going to stretch for another five. And it simply does not make sense to live in genteel poverty in an oversized but empty family home. Sure, the downside to reverse mortgages or selling the family home is that it could eat up the kids' inheritance, but the idea of retirees living in poverty seems silly to me. Sure, discuss it with the children, but no kids worth their salt would deny their parents quality of life in their retirement years.

WILLS

A valid will is simple and inexpensive, yet vitally important in ensuring that our estate goes to whomever we want, not some conniving, grasping relative, or – heaven forbid – the state. Amazingly, though, many Australians die every year without a will, even though it can be reasonably quick and easy to do one.

A will is a legal document stating what you want done with your possessions and property after your death. If you die without a will – known as dying 'intestate' – the probate division of the Supreme Court will decide what happens to your property in a process known as 'intestate succession'. Under this arrangement, with relatively minor variations between states, your property will pass first to your spouse, and if they don't exist, it goes to your children. Next in line are your relatives (in a specified pecking order), and so it goes on. If no close relatives can be found, it all ends up going into state coffers. This final fate is unlikely to reflect what you would have preferred if you had given the matter some thought and acted upon it earlier.

There are three ways of preparing a will – although the type of will that is right for you depends on the complexity of your financial affairs. You can have one drawn up by a solicitor, and this will cost from about $300 upwards. Solicitors will also administer the estate at your request, with their fees normally being deducted from the estate. The key reason for using a solicitor and paying the fee, of course, is that they ought to draw up a will that will unambiguously reflect your wishes, and stand up to any legal challenge from the vultures and ghouls circling about.

An alternative to using a solicitor is to use a trustee company. They come in two forms – state or public trustees, and private trustees. Generally there is little or no fee for writing the will, but the trustee retains the right to administer the estate. Naturally, there are fees for this, based on a percentage of the estate's assets, with the structure and size of fees varying across companies. These fees can be quite expensive, but where you are leaving a large estate, trustees can be worth their weight in gold. They are of most benefit when the estate is complicated and involves the long-term administration of a trust fund for your beneficiaries. They are also very useful if there are some sharks or generally difficult people among the beneficiaries.

Most of us with everyday financial affairs, though, can get by with something basic, and write our own will using a legal will kit. There are a number of good, inexpensive will kits around, normally sold through newsagencies. However, if you do it yourself, you need to be careful to fill it out correctly or it will be legally invalid.

As part of drawing up a will, you'll need to appoint an executor or two, whose job it is to administer your estate and to see your will is carried out as you intended. The executor is responsible for ensuring that all legal requirements relating to the estate are properly dealt with. Most importantly, they have the final say in any dispute over the will, short of a legal challenge.

Anyone can be an executor, including a beneficiary, a solicitor or a professional trustee. But, given the responsibilities they have, it's vital they be competent and, above all, trustworthy. Pick someone you know and trust implicitly, preferably your spouse or partner, a close family member or friend. In the event there is no one you consider suitable for the role, you can nominate a professional to do the job, either a private trustee or the public trustee.

Now, there's not much point in having a will if no one knows where it is. Just ask the would-be beneficiaries of reclusive, loony billionaire Howard Hughes. So, make sure one copy is in a safe place for yourself, and give another copy to your executor and/or solicitor. Similarly, if you have specific requests for your funeral arrangements, make sure your beneficiaries know the details so that your send-off can go according to plan.

Useful contacts

	Telephone	Web site
Australian Taxation Office	132 861	www.ato.gov.au
Centrelink	132 300	www.centrelink.gov.au
Department of Family and Community Services	1300 653 227	www.facs.gov.au
Department of Health and Ageing (Aged care information line)	1800 500 853	www.health.gov.au
Department of Veterans' Affairs (DVA)	133 254 Freecall: 1800 555 254	www.dva.gov.au

Allowable limits under the income test

Family situation	Allowable limit for a full pension	Maximum limit for a part pension
Single	Up to $116 per fortnight	Less than $1231 per fortnight
Couple	Up to $204 per fortnight	Less than $2056 per fortnight
Couple separated due to illness	Up to $204 per fortnight	Less than $2434 per fortnight

Source: Centrelink, as at March 2003.

Allowable limits under the assets test for homeowners

Family situation	Allowable limit for a full pension	Maximum limit for a part pension
Single pensioner	Up to $145 250	Less than $294 000
Couple (combined)	Up to $206 500	Less than $453 500
Couple separated due to illness	Up to $206 500	Less than $504 000

Source: Centrelink, as at March 2003.

Allowable limits under the assets test for non-homeowners

Family situation	Allowable limit for a full pension	Maximum limit for a part pension
Single pensioner	Up to $249 750	Less than $398 500
Couple (combined)	Up to $311 000	Less than $558 000
Couple separated due to illness	Up to $311 000	Less than $608 500

Source: Centrelink, as at March 2003.

Senior Australians tax offset

Family situation	Income threshold	Income at which the offset cuts out	Maximum amount of offset
Single	$20 000	$37 840	$2230
Married	$16 306 (or $32 612 per couple)	$29 122 (or $58 244 per couple)	$1602 per person
Married but separated due to illness	$18 883 (or $37 766 per couple)	$35 203 (or $70 406 per couple)	$2040 per person

Source: Australian Taxation Office, as at March 2003.

Income limits for the Commonwealth Seniors Health Card

Family situation	Annual income limits
Single	$50 000
Couple (combined)	$80 000
Couple separated due to illness	$100 000

Source: Centrelink, March 2003.

Staying ahead in tough times

Having almost come to the end of the book, I'm not going to pretend that all of our lives and our financial plans will work out in this type of sequence. And there are some experiences, such as unemployment, which I certainly hope you won't have to get through! But one message I want to get across is that if we want to live out our dreams, we have to pay for them. I know that many Australians are doing it very tough already on squeaky-tight budgets, but the vast majority of Australians are in a position where they can do a number of basic things that can lead to financial success.

Up to this point I've looked at ways to survive specific circumstances that we can find ourselves in. But I also reckon there are lots of other things we can do to build our wealth at any point in our lives. These days, money, or the lack of it, can bring on more headaches than just about anything else. Yet there is a lot we can do to make things easier, and to let us control our finances rather than the other way around.

Now, you may have noticed a number of recurring themes throughout this book, such as the importance of budgeting, saving and paying off your home as soon as possible. But there are loads of other little things we can do to reach financial independence, and this chapter is all about the reasonably simple steps that we can follow at any stage of our lives – during the good times and the not-so-good times, to help build our wealth.

There is nothing hard or complicated about the ideas you will find in this chapter, but the fact is that too few of us follow them. Most of us could manage our money a bit better, and doing so could mean having extra money to get rid of debts quicker or build your retirement nest egg. It just takes a bit of discipline and commitment to make it happen.

The earlier we start the easier it is, but no matter when you start, in my experience, nearly all of us can improve the situation we're in today, or take steps to greatly improve our future. Have a look at the ideas set out in this chapter. You may find you are already doing a lot of the things I mention here, and if that's the case, give yourself a pat on the back. Hopefully there will be some new ideas, or others you had forgotten about, and even if you follow just one or two, it's sure to set you on the road to wealth creation.

HAVE FINANCIAL GOALS

Money is not much good to you when you are dead. So, while I am very keen for you to have a vision about what it is you want to achieve financially and how you want to live your life in times to come, you can't forget about today. If you overspend today, your future looks glum. But if you underspend today and live like a reclusive monk, you may well achieve your long-term goals but not have any fun along the way, which would be very dull.

Somewhere between the two extremes lies the right strategy,

but you have to work that out for yourself. Providing that you are willing to work out your goals, actually achieving them is very possible. Lets face it, very few people are successful with their finances. People fret about money, look for shortcuts and hope to win Tattslotto – in fact, they do just about everything *except* what they should be doing, which is to set up some short, medium and long-term goals.

Let me tell you about a babysitter we used to have. She reckoned she couldn't save any money at all. Then one day she decided she wanted to go and live in Europe for a year and, of course, she needed some money to do that. Suddenly she could save. New clothes or going out every night seemed less important than achieving her goal. And as she gradually began to reach her goals, she was spurred on by her own success.

It's the same for all of us. We need to set goals because it is often the thrill of achieving them that keeps us going.

WORK TOWARDS YOUR GOALS

It is all very well to have plans, but unless you take steps to make your plans a reality, not much is going to happen. The following are some ideas to help you achieve your financial goals.

Save little, save often

I know I have spoken about this in other chapters of this book, but it is worth repeating. That's because savings are the bedrock of wealth, and while it is true that we can make savings in big areas by, say, trimming back on overseas holidays or designer-label clothes, it is also easy to make relatively small changes that simply become part of our lifestyle. Just think about all the 'treats' we buy ourselves, and not just once a week, but sometimes every day. I'm talking about things like a couple of beers after work, a packet of cigarettes, or takeaway food. The amounts you spend on these may not seem like much in themselves, but when you add them up they can amount to something quite big. However, the good news is that the pendulum can also swing the other way – you can turn a big spend into a big save.

For example, if you can save just $5 a day, you could accumulate over $1800 in a year. That's almost $2000 dollars extra, tax-free. If you're a traveller, it is the equivalent of an airfare to Europe. If you were in the market for clothes, it would pay for 25 pairs of Levi's jeans. It could also buy you around 60 new CDs.

That $5 a day could also be used to improve your financial well-being. And when you think about it, it's not too hard to trim your daily spending by $5. Now, I'm not suggesting you live a spartan existence. But it is getting started in a savings routine that is often the hardest part. Once you see your funds growing there is much more of an incentive to set aside part of your income.

Spend wisely

Not all of us have savings – but all of us spend. And we can all find ways to spend more sensibly.

Over many years of being involved with the *Money* show and *Money Magazine*, stories looking at ways of saving at the shops have always been very popular – and rightly so.

In Chapter 4 I pointed out that even seasoned budgeters often find themselves short anywhere between $50 to $300 each month. And the culprit is often shopping. There cannot be too many of us who haven't popped down to the shops for a loaf of bread and come home feeling rather sheepish about having spent a whole lot of dough. And let's face it – the odds of sticking to a shopping list are stacked against us. The marketing departments of some of our biggest retailers are constantly dreaming up new ways to get us to part with our money.

With around 14% of our weekly income spent on groceries, the supermarket is one place you can make some real savings. Impulse buying is a killer and retailers know it, so here are some inside tips on how to beat the retailers at their own game.

- Staples like eggs and milk are often placed at the back of the store, forcing you to pass through aisles of other goodies before you get to them. Exact your revenge by heading straight to what you want – and leave straight after.
- Be wary of 'complementation'. This is the practice of putting goods that complement each other on the same shelf space. You see it all the time – biscuits are opposite tea and coffee, pasta is located next to pasta sauces, and so on. Beat this trick by sticking to what you need.
- Expensive goods are often displayed on gondolas – these are the racks that adjoin the ends of aisles. They give every impression of being a bargain area, but if you compare prices you'll find that is usually not the case.
- Watch price scanners at the checkout and check your receipt. If you are overcharged on the shelf price at the supermarket, you are entitled to a refund.
- Every few months give the shopping a miss to use up those items lurking in the back of your cupboards or freezer.

One easy way to stretch your shopping dollar further is to visit the shops less often. There is no doubt that frequent shopping trips will add to your monthly bill because it is easy to buy a few extra items each time you visit the shops. In fact, a worrying trend these days is to regard shopping as a leisure activity. I am excluding myself from this, as I admit to finding shopping about as enjoyable as having a bull ant in my underpants. But for many people a love of shopping amounts to a love of spending, and it is a major contributor to high levels of personal debt.

Shopping for big-ticket items like furniture or white goods is an art form in itself. And the golden rule is never to pay full price.

Everything goes on sale eventually and if it isn't already marked down, try bargaining with the vendor. Ask if you can buy the floor model, which will usually be at a reduced cost, or offer to pay in cash.

Shop around for the best deal

Stretching your dollars is all about getting the best deal you can. And in most cases that means shopping around to get the best price. No matter what it is you are buying, you can't save unless you have a range of prices to compare from. Now, I would be the first to admit that shopping around for different prices involves time. But the good news is that it can often be done over the phone or via the Internet, and shopping around can mean the difference between paying full price for something and making big savings.

It never hurts to let a retailer know you are comparing their price to someone else's. Make it known you are looking for a good deal and you will often be offered a discount or some other sweetener.

Start looking at shopping as a necessity, not a leisure activity. Go shopping as little as possible – it is just too easy to buy extra items every time you go to the shops.

Remember cash is king

I reckon there's a lot to be said for paying in cash. After all, it wasn't all that long ago that if we wanted to buy an expensive item we saved for it or paid it off gradually using lay-by. But these days, it seems that the heyday of cash has well and truly ended. And that's a pity, because using cash can give you some real advantages. The most obvious is that it doesn't push you into hock, and when you have to save up for an item, you have plenty of time to think about whether or not you really want it.

Also, any shopkeeper will tell you that cash is king at the counter. You will always do your best deals with cash. For large items in particular, such as furniture and electricals, always negotiate for the best deal, then see if you can get an even better price by paying with cash. It's a fair bet you will because you're saving the retailer around 2% in credit card merchant fees.

Read the fine print

Once you sign a contract you are bound by the conditions contained in it, and even the most harmless-sounding contracts can contain clauses that could see you landing in hot water if you don't read and understand everything the contract says. Contracts don't make riveting reading but all too often people fail to read the fine print and it ends up costing them.

Contracts have certainly become more readable in recent years but never assume that your contract is 'standard' – especially if the person asking you to sign tries to convince you it is! It is generally in the small print that you will find the 'ifs' and 'buts' – all the reasons for not delivering the goods or money involved. The terms used in the contract may be simple enough, but unless you take the time to understand what is written, you risk losing money.

One of the basic rules of entering any contract is never to sign anything on the spot. Take the contract home for a few days, think it over and don't be afraid to ask questions if there is anything you don't understand – especially when things are couched in incomprehensible 'legal speak'. If you do come across a contract that you haven't fully read and understood, the golden rule is 'don't sign it'.

But contracts for the sale of goods or insurance aren't the only place you'll find fine print. Whether you are opening a new bank account or being asked to sign an agreement to act as guarantor on a loan, the fact is that you are presumed to have read everything you sign. So, the same rules apply. Regardless of who is asking you to sign, even if it is a friend or relative, don't be embarrassed to ask questions, and if you are in any doubt, get advice from a trusted third party.

Keep super for retirement

Thankfully, these days superannuation has become much more important in our lives than it has been in the past. We have gone from expecting to retire on a government-funded pension to planning ahead for our own financial wellbeing when we leave work. And as the balance of our super accounts grow, it can be enormously frustrating for anyone strapped for cash to see thousands of dollars sitting just out of reach in a superannuation fund.

But if you are aged less than 55 years there are tight regulations over when you can get early access to the preserved part of your super. You can only do so on the grounds of compassion or financial hardship. Just wanting to take a round-the-world trip doesn't quite cut the mustard!

Now, you can get in touch with your fund for more information but, as a guide, if you wish to claim on the grounds of extreme financial hardship, you need to show that you cannot meet reasonable costs of living and, in addition, you will need a statement from Centrelink showing that you have been in continuous receipt of Commonwealth income support for at least 26 weeks.

To make a claim on the grounds of compassion, you will need to be either undergoing medical treatment not available at a public hospital; having to meet the cost of modifications to your home or vehicle due to a severe disability; having to meet the costs of a funeral or palliative care; or needing funds for mortgage repayments where a mortgagee has threatened foreclosure.

As you can see, these are pretty tough conditions indeed and deliberately so, as the government is keen for us to contribute to the cost of our own retirement rather than relying on a public pension.

Protect your best assets

Life insurance Protect your best asset – you! You could probably argue that life insurance should be called 'death insurance', since that is what you are insuring against. And while you won't be around to reap the benefits of your policy, your dependants certainly will, which makes this type of insurance very important – especially if you are the household's main breadwinner.

There are two types of life cover available – 'term insurance' and 'whole of life'.

Term insurance In the event of your death, term insurance will provide your dependants with a lump sum. How much cover will you need? Many insurance agents suggest a reasonable figure is ten to 15 times the annual expenditure needs of your dependants. Others suggest anywhere between three to ten times your salary in addition to an amount necessary to cover your debts.

The size of the premium depends on the amount of cover you are looking for, but it is also determined by a combination of your age, your gender and your occupation. A 60-year-old male smoker who earns a living as a stuntman will pay far more than, say, a 30-year-old non-smoking woman who is a bank teller. Term insurance often requires you to undergo a medical examination.

Most policies will pay out if you die from illness and accident, but a general exclusion is if you commit suicide.

Many people will find they have an element of life cover with their super fund. While this is good news on one hand, there are some important considerations, the first being that the super fund trustee has the right to overrule your decision about who the beneficiary is. Secondly, if the payout goes to a beneficiary who is not a dependant of yours, they may be taxed on the payout, which won't happen if the life cover is provided through an insurance company.

The premiums for life insurance are not tax-deductible but nor is the payout taxable.

This is a competitive field of insurance with a large number of insurers vying for your business, so there is plenty of opportunity to shop around for the policy that suits you best. However, the Australian Securities and Investments Commission has issued a warning about life insurance policies being sold by telemarketers. Buying anything in this way gives you little or no chance to shop around, and in the case of life insurance, it could see you being sold a policy that doesn't match your needs.

Whole of life policies 'Whole of life' policies used to be very popular and many Australians still have one. But for my money, a term insurance policy is probably better value. Whole of life policies are made up of an insurance component as well as an investment component. Your premium, which is determined by your age when you take out the policy, stays the same until you die, or the policy matures, usually when you reach 60 or 65. If you die before this, the policy pays a predetermined amount, and if you are still around, you receive the investment component as a lump sum payout.

This is not a problem if the investment has performed well, but all too often the investment value of the policy is small once the life insurance company has taken its cut in fees and charges. Research has also shown that you could be better off buying a cheaper term policy and investing the cost difference yourself.

If you do have a whole of life policy, one simple way of determining whether or not you should keep it is to find out the cash value of your policy and compare it to your total contributions to date. If the cash value is close to the value of your contributions – or worse, if it is less – it may be time to cut your losses and pull out, as this is one investment that is not growing. Of course, finding out the cash value of your policy should be as simple as asking your insurance company, but you may well find yourself being given the run around, so be persistent and only accept the cash value of the policy, not the current value or any other figure.

There was a time when only the breadwinner of the family took out life insurance, but these days it is a good idea to insure the homemaker as well.

Income protection insurance Income protection insurance is a must if you are on your own (particularly if you are raising children), if you are paying off your own home or if you have other large borrowings. It will provide you with an income stream if sickness or injury mean you are unable to work in your normal job, with benefits normally being paid monthly, not as a lump sum. On the plus side, the premiums for income protection insurance are tax deductible, but on the downside, there is a limit to the amount of cover you can take out – usually around 75% of your monthly income. Before you start shopping around for the best deal, check that you don't already have cover through your superannuation fund, many of which have a group income protection policy.

There are a few traps for the unwary when it comes to income protection insurance, and the first is that while you may be tempted to go for a lower premium, it is likely to mean a longer waiting period before you get paid.

Broadly speaking, there are two types of contract offered for income protection. 'Agreed value' contracts are so named because the insurer pays you income of an agreed value, no matter what your current income is. These types of contracts are rapidly losing ground to 'indemnity' type contracts, where you are paid 75% of your income in the 12 months leading up to the claim. These are cheaper and they may be fine if you are on a salary, but they may not be the best option if you are self-employed or if your income is quite variable.

You will also come across two different definitions of disability. Under a 'duties' based policy, you should be entitled to a payout if you cannot perform the usual duties required in your line of work. Disability may also be defined according to your 'income'.

Here you are entitled to a payout if you are unable to earn a certain percentage of your previous income.

Some of the things that will determine the size of your premium include whether or not you want the benefits to be adjusted in line with inflation, and also your occupation. As you would expect, white collar workers can generally expect to pay lower premiums than blue collar workers due to a lower risk of injury. Some policies define employment to be any employment, including lower-paid unskilled work, so check that your policy will cover you if you cannot perform your regular job.

Set aside funds for emergencies

It seems we have a safety net of some sort to cover just about every aspect of our lives – for example, our cars are fitted with airbags to cushion us in the event of a crash – yet it is amazing how few of us have a cash reserve that we can fall back onto in a financial emergency.

Part of the problem is that we often gear our spending to our income levels. Any rises we have in our wages or salaries tend to go towards upgrading our lifestyle. The danger with this is that you are left extremely vulnerable in the event of a financial crisis. And sometimes the unexpected happens. It can happen to anyone. It can be anything from personal illness or accident to the loss of your job. Whatever the cause, without a cushion of emergency funds, a relatively minor hiccup in life can escalate into a full-blown catastrophe.

As a rule of thumb, it is a good idea to have a buffer of around three months' worth of living expenses set aside. This can be held in a term deposit, a cash management trust or an online bank account so that it still forms part of your portfolio. But the money is relatively accessible if you need it for an unforeseen event.

Keep your debt down

In Chapter 4, I looked at ways of getting out of debt. Hopefully this will give you some ideas about clearing your debts, but what is even better is not getting into hock in the first place. The use of credit these days is not only accepted – it is actively encouraged through the use of frequent spending and customer loyalty reward programs. But with Australia groaning under the weight of personal debt, we could do with relying on debt a lot less.

Paying bills

There is no doubt that when it comes to paying bills, your credit card can be very handy – especially if the money is a bit tight. However, using credit cards to pay bills brings only temporary relief. Eventually the full amount must be repaid – possibly with interest. Keeping on top of your regular bills is an important part of staying on top of your money. Here are some ideas on how to do it.

- Work out who in the household is responsible for paying bills and agree on a place where the unpaid bills will be kept.
- Check the due dates of each bill when you receive them and write them on a calendar. Circle the due date and cross them out as they fall due and have been paid.
- Set aside money to cover all your expenses for the month.
- Aim to pay your bills on time and get a receipt for them if you pay in cash.

Track down any missing money

According to the Tax Office, there is well over $4 billion sitting in 'lost super'. These are unclaimed balances in superannuation funds, and they come about when you change jobs or addresses. Even though the amounts may be small, retirement is a time when every penny counts. Any lost super belonging to you can be tracked down by getting in touch with the Tax Office 'lost members' hotline on 131 020.

There is also a few billion dollars worth of unclaimed money sitting in various government coffers around the country. The amounts cover everything from unclaimed dividends to share sale proceeds and it is well worth looking into these – especially as in many instances it can be done via the Internet. You will need to contact the office of state revenue (or treasury) in your state or territory for more information.

It's also worth investigating whether or not the Australian Securities and Investments Commission (ASIC) knows the whereabouts of any of your money. They have information on life insurance policies that have matured, shares or other money owing to you from companies as well as any forgotten bank, building society or credit union accounts. ASIC can be contacted on 1300 300 630.

Budget Planner

I reckon a budget is the single most important step to better money management. But, sadly, it's the first thing most people neglect. Now, I realise that it can be scary doing a budget to see how much of our hard-earned money slips through our fingers, but it's good medicine even if it tastes rotten. A budget helps us see where our money is going and once we know that, we can make adjustments in order to save some of it – which is vital, because if we don't save, we don't end up with anything.

Budgeting is a bit like dieting. For some people it just never works and despite the best intentions, you seem to put more on than you take off. And if you've tried budgeting and it hasn't worked in the past, it's probably because it wasn't realistic in the first place. Most people do a budget that's more appropriate to the life of a reclusive monk. But if your budget doesn't allow you to live it up a bit, you're not going to stick with it for very long.

So, draw up a budget if you don't already have one, and do allow it to let you have fun.

Here's how it's done. First complete the income column – and remember this is your after-tax income. Next, work out what you spend on each item weekly and annually. For example, if you pay home and contents insurance once a year, write that figure in the 'year' column and then divide it by 52 to calculate a weekly sum. Similarly, if you've got a figure for your weekly groceries bill, multiply by 52 to get a total for the 'year' column.

If you're unsure of your weekly outlay on things like groceries and petrol, keep a record of what you spend for a month or so and then work out an average.

Once your Budget Planner is complete and the numbers are added in each column, you'll have your totals for weekly and annual spending. But don't let the numbers put you off! The interesting bit comes next.

Take the amount you spent away from the amount you earned. Hopefully, you will have earned more than you spent! If you haven't, then at least your budget can show you where you can make some savings.

If the budget shows you've made more than you spent, it's time to make plans for investing this money to build your wealth. You could make extra payments off the mortgage or pay off your credit card. You could invest in shares or a managed fund, or you could save for a special purpose.

By drawing up a budget you've leapt an important financial hurdle – you've taken the first step in taking control of your finances. It's a small step but it makes a big difference!

	Per week	Per year
INCOME		
Your income after tax		
Your spouse/partner's income after tax		
Interest on savings		
Dividends on shares		
Investment property income		
Managed fund distributions		
Centrelink payments		
Other income		
TOTAL INCOME		
EXPENSES		
HOME		
Mortgage repayments/rent		
Telephone		
Mobile telephone		
Repairs and maintenance		
Furniture		
Appliances		
Rentals		
Other		
TOTAL		
MOTOR VEHICLE		
Registration		
Petrol		
Servicing and repairs		
Lease and loan repayments		
Other		
TOTAL		

	Per week	Per year
FOOD		
Groceries/milk/bread		
Meat		
Alcohol/cigarettes		
Eating out/takeaways		
Other		
TOTAL		
INSURANCE		
House and contents		
Health		
Motor vehicle		
Income protection		
Life insurance		
Other		
TOTAL		
FAMILY EXPENSES		
Education – school fees, uniforms, etc		
Child care		
Pets		
Sports		
Subscriptions and memberships		
Clothing		
Personal care		
Gifts		
Hairdresser/barber		
Entertainment		
Holidays		
Transport		
Other		
TOTAL		

	Per week	Per year
HEALTH		
Medical bills		
Dental bills		
Medicine		
Other		
TOTAL		
OTHER FINANCE		
Loan repayments		
Credit cards		
Store cards		
Lay-bys		
Superannuation		
Donations		
Other		
TOTAL		
TOTAL EXPENSES		
TOTAL INCOME		
TOTAL EXPENSES		
MONEY YOU COULD BE SAVING*		
(Total income less total expenses)		

*If this figure is negative, that is, your income is *less* than your expenses, you are spending more than you earn. And that means it is time to cut back. Look for areas in your budget where you could reduce your spending – likely categories are entertainment, eating out and other non-essentials.

Debt Tracker

Sometimes your debts are seemingly insurmountable, but you'd be surprised at how often a simple solution can help the problem. The trick is to tackle the problem logically, looking at all the issues involved and then going to a lender with a detailed, written proposal.

All too often, people in a financial mess approach their bank in an emotional, disorganised state, and are then surprised when the bank says 'No'. The banks really don't like taking stern action, but you must approach them in a professional, businesslike fashion.

That's where the Debt Tracker (see page 221) comes in. The aim of it is to help you take an organised approach in your dealings with lenders.

When it comes to managing your debts or renegotiating your repayments, the first step is to write down everything you owe. List the high-interest debts first and work your way down to the balances with the lowest interest rate. If you can pay off the more expensive, high-interest amounts first, you'll cut back on your overall interest bill.

The next step is to approach each of your lenders with a suggested repayment plan. This means doing a bit of homework beforehand to work out what you can afford to pay on each of your debts. Whenever any new repayments or terms are agreed upon with a lender, keep a record of whom you spoke to and when, recording it on the Debt Tracker. Repeat whatever has been agreed upon back to the person you are dealing with so that you are both clear on what was decided. If there is anything you are unsure of or that you don't understand, you really need to get it sorted out. And always ask for any new arrangements to be put in writing.

Remember, how soon you can get rid of all your debts depends on how disciplined you are in keeping up with the repayments. A creditor may be willing to renegotiate once, but if you fail to keep up with the new repayments they are unlikely to lend a sympathetic ear the second time round.

If a creditor or lender won't budge on the repayments, get in touch with the Department of Fair Trading, or Consumer Affairs, in your state. It may be possible to get a court order that sets out a new repayment schedule if you're in a position of real hardship. For more information on this, take a look at Chapter 4.

Debt Tracker

Creditor's name and phone number	Account number	Interest rate	Loan security	Balance owed	Payment due date	Original repayment	Amount of last payment	New agreed repayment	Date of first payment	Name of contact person

Index